Exploring Native American Wisdom

Wisdom

Lore, Traditions, and Rituals That Connect Us All

EXPLORING NATIVE AMERICAN WISDOM

Lore, Traditions, and Rituals That Connect Us All

By
Fran Dancing Feather
and
Rita Robinson

NEW PAGE BOOKS
A division of The Career Press, Inc.
Franklin Lakes, NJ

EXPLORING NATIVE AMERICAN WISDOM
EDITED AND TYPESET BY NICOLE DEFELICE
Cover design by Diane Y. Chin
Printed in the U.S.A. by Book-mart Press

To order this title, please call toll-free 1-800-CAREER-1 (NJ and Canada: 201-848-0310) to order using VISA or MasterCard, or for further information on books from Career Press.

The Career Press, Inc., 3 Tice Road, PO Box 687,
Franklin Lakes, NJ 07417
www.careerpress.com
www.newpagebooks.com

Library of Congress Cataloging-in-Publication Data

Dancing Feather, Fran.
    Exploring Native American wisdom : lore, traditions, and rituals that connect us all / by Fran Dancing Feather and Rita Robinson.
      p. cm.
    Includes index.
    ISBN 1-56414-625-1 (pbk.)
      1. Indians of North America—Religion. 2. Indian philosophy. 3. Conduct of life. I. Robinson, Rita. II. Title.

E98.R3 D136 2003
299'.7—dc21
                                               2002071905

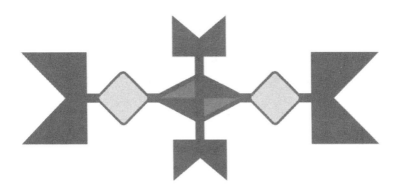

Dedication

Gratitude for this book is given back to our extended families and the Creator.

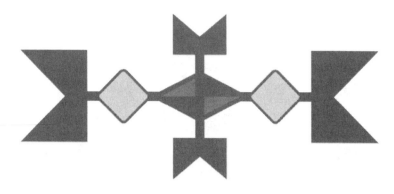

ACKNOWLEDGMENT

As well as friendship, Rita and I have worked together for several years on our own writing, but this was our first attempt to write a book together. Without our collaboration, and her introduction to Senior Acquisitions Editor Michael Lewis at Career Press/New Page Books, this book would not have been possible.

—Fran Dancing Feather

Through the years of friendship with Fran Dancing Feather, I've come to know and respect Native American culture and traditions. It was pure pleasure to work with her, and to absorb even more knowledge and practical life-enriching experiences. The two of us would also like to thank Editor Nicole DeFelice of Career Press/New Page Books for her fine editing.

—Rita Robinson

Contents

INTRODUCTION

Native Americans witnessed and took part in a rebirth of their traditional ways during the last half of the 20th century. After decades of turmoil, they began to seek the wisdom of the few elders who were still alive after the reservation era ended. They stopped fighting to regain lost freedom and turned to ancient knowledge. Secretly, they learned to pray and seek vision the old way. The journey was slow and long. They discovered that no matter what life had handed them, they could find peace within, and bring the supernatural world of their ancestors back to life.

So successful have they been in showing the world how to overcome adversity that seekers in other cultures turn to them in order to understand the sacredness of Mother Earth, respect for all living things, and their own place and strength in the circle of life.

This sweet wellspring of the spiritual taught many Native Americans how to live successfully in a rapidly changing world, while reopening the ancient door to the divine power and wisdom in each of us.

This divine power and wisdom involves a mystical dimension where humans can communicate with animals, fire, wind, water, earth, and each other more effectively.

The increasing need to discover an independent personal power, protection, and sense of individuality calls us to seek the wisdom of not only the ancients, but the wisdom of the elders in pursuit of a supernatural experience in our daily lives.

Why was I born? Why must I die? What is my purpose in this life? How can I interact with the universe? What are my talents and gifts? Are there really visions? Is there a Deity? Before we can understand spiritual development, we must come to understand ourselves.

The First Americans who lived in the Golden Age of Prehistory had the same questions. Natives then and now follow the same traditional path to understanding of self and the supernatural through vision quests, dreams, ceremonies, honoring our ancestors and living elders, and exploration of natural laws.

We can discover our divine selves by a series of native activities that call on inner vision and secrets waiting in our hearts to come alive. United with the free gifts of the earth, we enter a mystical dimension of self-discovery and union with the oldest Spirit of Creation. This wisdom of the Old Ones shows us our own uniqueness and unravels the mysteries of sanctity already waiting inside us that can burst forth like living water to nourish the cornfield of the spirit.

Fears of death and financial insecurity become obsolete as we learn to trust ourselves in all areas of our lives, from earnings to our healing powers.

We discover inner talents and gifts as we journey to the top of the sacred mountain to meet Eagle, who flies us to a new dimension filled with energy and power, leaving the mundane behind.

Enemies become worthy opponents. Pain becomes purification, and strife disappears. There are no problems, only challenges when we discover that everything is sacred and that our souls are very old. Trudging becomes dancing as we gain the strength and perseverance to make our lives new each day. No matter what our job or position in this life, we have the ability to change the journey from one of drab, gray boredom to one of colorful discovery.

As history has moved forward into the new millennium, we see the ways of the Native American life as that of the resurrected warrior. How did this happen, and how did Native Americans make the journey?

They learned to adjust to a new world, and to share their ancient wisdom with others.

Everyone can tap into their own wealth of ancient wisdom using Native American ways. The road may not be easy, but it is well worth the effort, because it fosters a richer and more abundant life.

1

DISCOVERING YOURSELF IN A NATIVE WAY

The "native path" or "red road" does not refer to any particular tribal tradition, because each of the approximately 700 American Indian tribes in the United States maintain practices that are unique to their particular group or family. Many more tribes, some of whom are related to Native Americans, exist south of the border and also practice ancient tradition.

For this reason, there is no one way to walk the old ways of the ancestors, but many.

The "old ways"

In an effort to understand and define the various collective beliefs of native people, 50 individuals from different tribal groups came together in 1978 to form the Indian Child Welfare Act, part of which summarizes traditional cultural value preferences. It explains Native Americans' relationship between "man, nature, and the environment."

In essence, it was determined that native people:

☞ Desire to seek harmony with nature, rather than control it.

☞ Choose the present to be more important than the future.

☞ Believe that humans are basically good rather than evil.

☞ Emphasize communal or clan lifestyle rather than individual status and priorities.

☞ Place greater value on spiritual accomplishments, as opposed to materialism.

☞ Respect other religions, and avoid proselytizing.

The study helped Native Americans and others to understand themselves, their relationships to ancestry, and the changing environment in which they now live. It also helped them retain their traditions while living successfully in a world that is sometimes at odds with the contemplation, respect, and silence that they value. These values are available to people in all cultures who want their world to become more harmonious. It begins by paying homage to their ancestors and elders.

Who are your ancestors?

Spirituality encompasses every area of native life, and family values are held in high esteem. We honor our elders and ancestors. We also honor the elders of all cultures, because they are filled with many valuable lessons, the same as our own native elders.

Older relatives from all cultures have survived many decades of change. History has passed before their eyes. They are keepers of ancient wisdom.

Not so long ago, elders lived with their extended families until they died. They were treated very differently than they are now because they were very needed and full of wisdom. They helped with the little ones, so parents did not need to send their children to outside caregivers.

Educating children was filled with the rich traditions and moral teachings of the wisest people on the planet, their grandparents. The elders were cherished because of the help they gave to young parents.

They always knew the best old recipes for everything, and told wonderful stories about the days gone by. Children were fascinated by their wizened old grandmas and grandpas who had the wonderful gift of patience with them. They did not push them to learn fast and to overachieve. They had other priorities, such as teaching the importance of a spiritual life.

We all have these wonderful old folks in our families, although things have changed in today's fast-paced world. Elders of all cultures often live great distances from their children or grandchildren, or they become unable to care for themselves, and are placed in nursing facilities. But this needn't stop us from unlocking their treasure chest of wisdom by asking them questions and respecting their stories.

Our elders, no matter where they come from, rich or poor, fat or skinny, pretty or homely, soft or sharp, loud or quiet, are filled to the brim with our family heritage.

As we make contact with the elders in our families, it's a good idea to:

☞ Apologize if necessary for any hurts from the past.

☞ Bring a small gift to lift their spirits (it is Native American protocol to bring a small gift when seeking wisdom or other information).

☞ Write down a few questions before the visit in order to stay focused.

☞ Be open-minded, because it's very possible that the family, like others, has its own dysfunction, alienation, or other wreckage to deal with.

☞ Be good listeners, but steer them away from negative conversation.

☞ Keep a positive outlook.

Ask about their lives, not their health

If we just ask our elders how they are doing, especially if they are in a nursing home, we're likely to get a litany of aches and pains, and tales of the terrible food they've been subjected to. But if we ask them questions about their younger days, their eyes light up, and they often paint wonderful pictures of their lives, which is really the touchstone of our own lives.

They know how to sustain many decades of marriage to the same person, and to love them just as much when they die as they did the day they were married. They understand how to endure the most devastating tragedies life can dish out. If we listen closely, they will tell us how they survived it all. The women elders can even tell a 50-year-old woman how to survive menopause with dignity better than a gynecologist.

They know how to cook without a microwave, sew without a machine, discipline and reward children, celebrate the holidays the old way, recycle better than today's environmentalists, and often play a musical instrument to boot.

Making peace

Every effort we undertake to make peace with our elders will be rewarded in ways we never imagined. Still, it can be a difficult journey for many of us who have been estranged from them.

Others of us maintain close, sweet relationships with the old ones, but we may never have asked them about things that will bring out their wisdom.

It is not appropriate to think our families have no culture. Every family comes from somewhere.

I worked with a non-native woman, a physician of 20 years, whose family comes from the Midwest. She went home to learn about her elders, thinking she wouldn't get much out of it. As she drove through the rolling landscape, she was overcome by the delightful feminine energy she felt from the countryside. She wrote about all these feelings in her journal.

By the time she reached her parent's home, she had written 11 pages about the beauty of the farm country of her birth. Without realizing it, she had already begun to seal the bond with her people.

She returned home a few weeks later with a new attitude. I had suggested she visit the grave of her ancestors, in order to understand her heritage from those who had passed on. She was to spend time alone near their graves in silence to touch their spirits and let them sink into her soul.

She was to watch and observe her parents as though they were strangers, asking questions and believing the answers, no matter what they said.

Her questions concerned what they thought about God and politics, and current events. She did not interrupt when they answered. She wrote everything down in her journal before she slept each night during the visit. Journaling each day is necessary because the overload of information is too much to trust to memory.

She let them teach her without judging them, or allowing wreckage from the past to influence her. She looked five years younger when she returned—a changed woman.

We gain peace within ourselves, and gain a true sense of our own identity when we respect older family members. Our parents and grandparents are a huge part of who we are, and so is the location of where they live or lived, just as it is important to know our own birthplace, and where we were raised. If our grandparents or great-grandparents aren't living, we can direct questions about them to our parents or other family members.

Questions to ask

- ☞ Why did your parents/grandparents/great-grandparents come to live where they did?
- ☞ What country were the ancestors (maybe going back farther) from originally?
- ☞ What were their favorite books and other reading materials?
- ☞ What sort of music did they like?
- ☞ What type of artwork did they prefer?
- ☞ Were any of them creative?
- ☞ What were their religious or spiritual beliefs?
- ☞ Who was their favorite family member?
- ☞ Who was the most outlandish, wealthy, eccentric, artistic, grumpy (pick other characteristics, good or bad)?
- ☞ What type of work did they do (farmers, warriors, clergy, explorers)?
- ☞ What are some of their most vivid memories?

☞ Am I anything like them in my tastes, man-
nerisms, profession, and relationships?

☞ Can I please have some old family recipes and/
or home healing remedies?

The questions aren't geared to find out about the family tree. It's fine to know all the existing branches, but
what needs to be uncovered are stories that provide insight into what your people are all about.

These initial questions are the early beginnings of our
self-discovery. As we step into the roller-coaster ride of
our past, we need to hold on because it can be a very emotional ride.

Sharing the information

Now that the journey home has borne fruit, it's time
to share the treasure of your people. Although that initial
journey yielded abundant information, once the contact is
made, the exchange with your elders is neverending. It
becomes a lifelong quest, even if the journey was a rough
one. And we need to keep asking questions, and bringing
gifts as we seek out other elders in the family.

Serving up your dumplings

As a Native American, I had never tasted dumplings
in my entire life until one day when I was asked to a
friend's house for dinner. The family was from another
culture, and one of the old family recipes was chicken
and dumplings.

To someone who has never seen a dumpling, they look
very strange, indeed. As I scrutinized the unfamiliar round
thing on my plate, I prayed that I would be able to at least
swallow a small part of it so I wouldn't hurt the hostess's
feelings. To my surprise, it was incredibly good. I wound

up eating more than I was comfortable with because they were so delicious!

It reminded me of how our family ate fry bread every Sunday when I was a child. I always thought fry bread was "poor food" for Indians who couldn't afford anything else. We never served it to company. It was nothing to be proud of 40 years ago. Now it's considered a skill to be able to prepare fry bread the "old way." Also, these days, fry bread booths at native gatherings make more money than any other goods offered. When we eat it at home now, we joke about it being an "exotic ethnic delight."

As it turns out, some of the more seemingly inconsequential things our families take for granted become the greatest treasures of all. Older methods of cooking and serving meals to large families were often healthier than the meals we eat today, because they were fresher and free of pesticides. Fruit may have been picked from trees, and berries gathered on mountainsides.

So when we journey with our elders about the way they used to obtain their foods, it becomes not only rich in personal meaning, but also meaningful to our lives today.

By sharing these treasures from our elders we serve up our own cultural dumplings. We can do this by using old recipes from our family when we have company. Eating food is more than nourishment for the body. It nourishes the soul when we display the gifts of our heritage with others.

Strengths and beauties of your culture

For years I was self-conscious of my large Indian nose. As an adult, when I reclaimed my heritage, and quit trying to look non-native by dying my hair blonde, wearing heavy makeup, and never mentioning that I had been raised on a reservation, I became proud of my nose, as I became proud of my heritage.

You might ask yourself, "Where did this nose come from? Can I trade it for a smaller one? Why do I have these freckles?" Physical characteristics mark our families with distinct features and traits. Many other traits are formed by environmental influences, but many more are the result of genetics.

When a baby is adopted, the personality is formed partly by the adoptive family. Many times, however, when the child (as an adult) is reunited with birth family members, the similarities between them are striking. A pair of twins separated at birth were reunited in their 40s after one of them became obsessed with finding her sister. On meeting, they found both wore their hair exactly the same way, they weighed within two pounds of one another, and they shared many of the same habits and fears. This is only one of thousands of such cases of twins reunited after being raised by different families. Medical researchers study these siblings extensively, because they add validity to genetic traits that cannot be denied.

Straight or curly hair, eye color, skin color, height, bone size, weight, allergies, and tendencies toward chronic conditions (such as diabetes, longevity, addictions, hyperactivity or lethargy) are only a few of the strengths and weaknesses that family members share.

Full-blooded native people in North America are noted for their thick black hair, dark brown eyes, and olive or dark complexions. Separate tribes and extended families are often identified by more finely detailed similarities as well. For instance, people whose ancestors spent generations in the warm lower desert elevations of the southwest have bodies much like those of their ancestors, regardless of where they now live. They are often more heavyset, darker-skinned, and not as tall as those whose people originated in higher mountainous areas. Darker skin is less likely to sunburn, so is better suited to desert regions. Mountain people are generally lighter skinned and taller.

It is the same for people in all areas of the world. My niece Christina comes from Denmark. The weather there is much cooler than in the southwestern United States, where her dad (my brother), Pete, hails from. His ancestry is from two Indian groupings whose extended family migrated from the East Coast to Southern California prior to his birth. Pete is about six feet tall with black hair, dark brown eyes, and olive skin. He has the large family nose, and full lower lip, both characteristics of his clan.

Christina's mom, a native of Denmark, is tall, blonde, light complexioned, and slim. Pete and Christina live with her in Denmark. The sun in Denmark, in the Northern Hemisphere, is always south of earth, and never straight above the earth during the day. Natives of that country do not require as much skin pigmentation to protect them from those areas closer to the equator. Although Christina has some of her father's facial characteristics, she is lighter like her mother.

When Christina was 18, her dad brought her to the United States to visit her Native American relatives. We included her in ceremonies, and the old traditional practices and customs of our people. She met her brown cousins, ate native food, and came away with some of the richness of half of who she is to take home to Denmark. She's comfortable with who she is, because she knows her culture from both sides of the family.

Some aren't so lucky. We are too frequently influenced by the models we see in the media. We see native people who bleach their hair, and who work hard to achieve the physical characteristics of non-Indian people in an effort to fit in. Many of these same people, just as I did, lean toward their native culture as they get older and begin to seek their spirituality. Also, many non-natives who admire Indian culture try to copy it by darkening their hair and wearing Indian clothes.

What I have found to be true, though, is that when we embrace the roots of our own cultures (there may be more than one), it makes our lives richer, finer, and more complete. Then we are more capable and ready to embrace traditions of other cultures, and to learn from them.

Blending tribes

People have continually blended their cultures. In Southern California before the white man arrived, the tribes were mostly peaceful hunter-gatherers in an area rich in natural foods and resources. The coastal tribes were fishermen, and the mountain and desert tribes were hunters. Gatherings among them took place all over California, and our Creation story, still told today, was sung through the "bird songs," which could take up to three days to sing. The bird songs are stories of how to interact with one another—the four-legged, the winged ones, and the plants and rocks.

After the Spanish arrived, the natives were split into Mission Tribes, renamed and taught to speak Spanish and practice Catholicism. Later, when Americans took over, English became the native's language, so many natives spoke three languages.

My ancestors migrated west three generations ago from the east. We landed in California, confused about who owned Indian country. So a portion of my family speaks a few words of the original native language, some speak fluent Spanish, and nearly everyone speaks English. The result, sometimes, is a pigeon English, laced with words that may be Iroquois, Delaware, or Spanish. No one really knows.

This is how some of my tribesmen have emerged from this multi-assimilation. Some of our ceremonies have taken the same sort of beating.

The first combination of spiritual practices took place during a marriage in my family between two native tribes. We still sing songs from both of those tribes. During the migration of the family, my great-grandmother spent some time at Taos Pueblo in New Mexico, where she picked up some of their tribal ways. After arriving in California, half the family was converted to Catholicism during the reservation era. At age 11, I was sent from my California home to live in Navajo country in New Mexico, so some of their traditions rubbed off on me. Plus, the family has lived in California for five generations, so many of our traditions and our ways come from the local tribes. In my own life, I have lived on two different Indian Reservations, neither of which were my own tribal land.

Much of my family history and that of many other Native Americans who were born in California is recorded in the artwork and historical artifacts of the California Missions. Religious paintings and sculptures in the 200-year-old buildings were done with native dyes. The fathers were taught the herbal remedies, basket making, cooking, and food-gathering techniques that would help them survive in their new environment. Some Indian spirituality also rubbed of on the fathers, and the Missions to this day combine the spiritual symbols of Catholicism with heavy Native American influence.

A great many Americans, other than natives, have backgrounds of mixed ancestry. As confusing as it may appear, every form of lineage has very old and awesome qualities. Even if a person's family history isn't linked to a location, such as the Missions of California, reference books, gravesites, family homes, and heirlooms can all attest to a person's heritage. And the elders are often an untapped source of wonderful information. I've introduced my children to this world of the Missions, because it is a part of their personal history, skills, and spirituality.

Your Creation story

Mankind has studied human behavior ever since the first writings were carved on leaves, the walls of caves, and on stone tablets. These observations, which have traveled through thousands of years like an eternal river of souls, are as true today as they were in the time of White Buffalo Calf Woman, Moses, Pharaoh, and Sidhartha. People the world over have always sought to understand the nature of reality or Creation, and where it originated.

Every culture has fashioned a Creation story that has been passed down from generation to generation through verbal or written communication. The surviving religions of today's world each emphasize the importance of a spiritual life, as opposed to one centered on materialism.

Once we embrace our own individual Creation stories we begin to understand the motives, fears, and graces of our own ancestors along with an appreciation of how they got the way they are today. What moves our people, yours and mine? What do they fear and how do they reckon with it?

Many religions and faiths reflect the struggle between the dark side and the ultimate good of man. It is the very nature of us to encounter this struggle in the fabric of our lives. Many of the greatest and most compassionate leaders and heroes in history practiced a spiritual life. Maybe not like yours or mine, but spiritual.

A human being in native tradition cannot reach greatness without drawing power from the Greatness of All Things, or a Universal Order of Creation. To explore Native American wisdom, we need to open our minds to the various age-old ideas about Creation and discover for ourselves how to interpret them.

Defining our life's quest

The idea of embarking on any spiritual path is born of curiosity about our fullest potential. By turning our attention to the ancestors of our extended families or of our roots, we can understand deeper definitions of who we really are and why we are this way.

Native people hold great reverence for the teachings of the first Americans. We ask who our oldest relations are. We understand that they have already endured all the hardships we will ever need to know as we travel through today's world. So to define our purpose and the passions of this life, this is where we need to begin. We explore our roots, as we believe anyone who wants to understand native ways should.

We feel pride when we share the wisdom left to us by our elders. Once we know something about our people and their places of origin we can begin to practice the native concept of the "giveaway," the most profound act of sharing our physical, mental, and spiritual elements with others. This act of generosity, which can also include material possessions (such as food, crafts, and sacred objects), draws people from other cultures to us, and we see them begin to share a part of themselves. This gesture adds to the wisdom from which we draw as we begin the path of self-discovery that helps us define our quest in this life.

Discovering your own heritage

The term *red road* permeates the path of self-discovery native people take to understand themselves as their ancestors understood themselves. If non-natives want to take part and understand this red road, they may use the same methods our people have used to discover their heritage. All cultures, societies, and ethnic groups must learn to be proud of who they are, and from where they evolved. At the same time, we need to respect and understand the ways of other cultures and other native peoples.

☞ Discovering yourself in a native way is an opportunity to look at life from a different cultural perspective. We begin to define our priorities from a native point of view.

☞ We see ourselves as members of a clan or extended family, rather than individuals with no roots.

☞ We contact family members and embark on a quest of our own family lineage. What nationality or nationalities are we?

☞ We understand that our own cultural diversity is really who we are in a native way. Who we are makes us special and beautiful.

☞ Who are our people? What were they like? What characteristics made them unique? We learn their philosophies and something of their spiritual and political beliefs. Through this, we begin to understand more about ourselves and our own potential. Our minds and hearts begin to open for those who have gone before us.

☞ What are the strengths and beauties of your personal culture? What do we have as a result of our genealogy? Are we proud of our personal appearance and other characteristics shown by our inherited traits?

☞ Learn the Creation story or stories of your people. Have the stories evolved? Have they been replaced by a new Creation story? If so, does the new one suit your family? Does it work in today's world for you? Discover how and why.

☞ Discover the land where your people began their history. Find out how and why they moved to their present location, and what struggles they endured in order to survive. Were they assimilated into another society? If so, how did this assimilation affect them? Our land of origin, and the changes that occur when an assimilation or change of location takes place tells us much about how we became who we are today.

☞ Once we have researched our own people, we serve up something of them (we serve up our dumplings) to our friends in the form of meals, gifts, and stories. This helps us to build our own brand of "native pride."

2

THE POWER OF THE CIRCLE

All things good and true take place within the circle. It is the center of our spirituality. All is spherical.

No beginning and no end

The circle, or an adaptation of the circle, such as an oval, is the most common shape in the universe. The galaxy, which contains our solar system, moves out from the center of itself in a circular motion. The solar system moves in circular motion as well. Planets orbit the sun in a circle, just as neutrons and protons circle the nucleus of the atom.

The womb forms a sort of circular container where the life of every human begins. Trees are circular, and the various rings in their trunks record their history and age.

The compass is a circular form of measurement determining directions by a magnetic needle turning freely 360 degrees as it pivots to search for "true north."

To encompass is to embrace a focal point within your circle. What is true north and why seek it? True north is the focus—the goal—of the compass. To that same end, humans need to focus on their ultimate goal, or their "true north."

Understanding the purpose of the circle

An understanding of the circle, helps us to discover which part of that circle is truth for us.

Some who walk a spiritual path, whether it be Native American or another, refer to the "top of the mountain" as the spiritual goal or the "true north." Both are metaphors for the life goal of our journey. It becomes part of the circle. We each determine our top of the mountain through an evolving journey. The more we learn, the more insight we gain into a spiritual understanding of our personal circle. Through our journey we are able to find true north at the top of our very own sacred mountain.

A modern holy man talked about the many things we expect of ourselves in this life. He said our priorities are split in many directions, making it difficult to determine which priority holds the most importance. During his talk, he abruptly turned to one side, raised his hand upwards, and spoke more loudly, "Keep your eyes focused on the mountain." To this holy man, and to many others who seek spiritual enlightenment, the mountain is the Creator, the focal point of the circle.

Family circle

We embrace many circles in our lives, such as the "family circle." At the center of many families sits a patriarch or matriarch. This is usually a dominate older family member who assumes much of the responsibility for the extended family. If this person has appropriate communication skills and considerable love and compassion, he or she may generate a huge influence over a great number of people in the family circle. Such people spend a significant amount of time examining their own motives and contemplating how to help younger members of the family. Many of these Native American family leaders are very spiritually motivated as they teach and nurture the younger folks.

My husband and I have attended many native gatherings where the hot topic is "eldership." Leading a family spiritually, financially, and psychologically is a very sobering responsibility. It requires keeping up with the times, while sticking to traditional values. Excellent listening and counseling skills are needed.

Humility becomes a valuable tool for compassionate eldership, especially when one understands that "humility" and "humiliation" are not the same. Humiliation is a negative experience, but spiritual humility is a gift, even though it often becomes a challenge to maintain.

Humility is a positive type of faith in the ultimate rightness of things. It agrees with the Native American belief that the nature of us is authentically good, pure, and seeks love as a final goal. Humility is a quiet, courageous strength that gives the gift of empowerment and love to its adherents.

Humility is essential for leading others in the family circle toward peaceful living on life's terms. Strong, humble elders can hold a huge family together. The effects of their leadership can last for many generations after they die through a legacy of traditional values.

These elders can be male or female, father, mother, grandfather, or grandmother. But it's important to recognize and honor elders because they will enrich your life.

Circle of friends

A circle of friends is the circle we create of our own choosing. Pop culture dictates that we need to create a circle of friends healthy for us. "Stick with the winners," is a good thought. This is not a new concept for Native Americans, who, prior to contact with Europeans, were directed to live clean, healthful, moral lives from the time they were children.

Those who were productive, well adjusted, and happy were sought out by all. It is the same today. If we place ourselves in the company of those whose lives are a good example of healthful living, we are likely to pick up those traits and incorporate them into our lives.

On the other hand, if we spend a great deal of time with those who harshly criticize us out of resentment, or who have negative or dark outlooks on life, we are influenced by them as well.

Friends need not always agree about everything, but should show mutual respect for one another, and for each other's boundaries. Friends are those folks we feel safe with, and who do not drain us of time, money, or other resources.

Friendship can be split into three different types of categories if we want to be more clear about friendship.

☞ **Mentors** are those we look up to, and from whom we may wish to seek advice on anything from finances to spirituality. They walk slightly ahead of us in wisdom we want to absorb. Many native people seek out mentors. As a way to show respect for their wisdom, we make some sort of offering in exchange for their advice. When we go to them, it is customary to take them a small gift of something we believe might please them, such as certain foods they like, a small spiritual token, or even an inexpensive expression of honor. We do not embarrass them with extravagant or expensive gifts just to make a big show of our esteem for them. That would be inappropriate.

☞ **Peers** are those like-minded individuals we enjoy spending leisure time with. There may be a small amount of competition involved, but nothing really serious. We nurture give-and-take relationships with them, and seek to be self-actualizing. When we go places with them, sometimes we pick up the tab and sometimes they do. We are on equal ground with peers. We tell them the truth about ourselves. Other times we are asked to tell the truth about them. These folks are usually a lot of fun for us to be around, and we may share a lifetime of experiences with them. Some become best friends.

☞ **Seekers** are those who come to us for mentoring. We listen carefully as they try to tell us what they think they need. We may encounter them at work, or in some kind of volunteer organization. Many times, those who come to us for help are quite needy. We understand this and try to guide them to resources that can be of help. We do not sacrifice ourselves in a way that is harmful to us or our families. We listen and sometimes make suggestions, but we do not become codependent with them by taking on their problems as our own. My husband and I have made ourselves and our home available for years to help others. We know, though, that it is one thing to feel compassion, and another to inadvertently become involved in the problem, which is a huge mistake. We have discovered that carefully defining the different relationships in our circle of friends is imperative for balance.

Circle of the body

The circulatory and respiratory systems move in circular fashion throughout the body and the organs. They are constantly picking up the support they need and use to sustain life. Breathing picks up oxygen from the lungs and carries it around to every part of us. It fuels the blood and brain every moment of our lives. The blood takes essential nourishment from the small intestine where it begins the incredible journey into the metabolism of each cell and system throughout the body. These systems take in what they need and return to their true north where they expel waste products and cast off toxins that would kill us without their activity. This is an amazing form of the sacred circle of life. How this happens all by itself remains one of the greatest mysteries of our existence.

The nervous system moves around too, picking up stimulus from the physical senses. It carries the information to the brain where it is processed, and a response is delivered back through the nerves to the autonomic and voluntary nervous systems. As long as we are alive, it is a continuing circle of action with each action dependent on the action of another, and each, in turn, providing action to another.

Circle of the food chain

The circle of the food chain is the arrangement of organisms in an ecologically balanced environment. According to the nature of predation, each species uses the one who is the next lower member of the chain as its food source. This circle of the food chain recycles everything in its food path. So it stands to reason that each species within its chain will eventually become every other species in its earthly environment. This consumption is continuous without beginning or end.

Because we humans are dependent on this food chain, or circle of life, we give thanks to the animal killed for sustaining us, as well as giving thanks to the Creator. Our ancestors and those on reservations today make use of every part of that animal, for not only food, but clothing, shelter, and art, because it is a way of honoring the animal.

Circle of time

Native wisdom also sees time as being circular. The sundial and the clock are round. Time circles us in many concentric cycles. We may see the beginning of the 24 hours each day as a good example. It begins as daybreak, running its course through morning, afternoon, evening, night, and back around to daybreak in this continuing circle. Natives have always observed and measured time from moon to moon. We know that women follow a monthly physical cycle, so it is referred to as their "moon cycle."

The separate moons of the yearly cycle are significant because they mark the place of individual seasons. In the season of the moon when snow blows wild, like spirits dancing in the wind, we may think of January. Or in the season when Bear wakes from the sacred dreams, we know that it is May. It is so every year, every season, every lifetime. So it is circular.

Moving clockwise

All things that seek harmony with natural law move in clockwise motion. If we observe native people doing the friendship dance, we see that they dance the way the hands move around the circular face of the clock. As they dance this way, they create the sacred circle of life. They hold hands in a circle and dance sideways around the arena to bring together all people from separate tribes and extended families. It is a single ceremony of friendship. This usually happens at the beginning of a native gathering and serves to bring us all together in unity.

The universe moves clockwise, and the planets circle the sun clockwise. The earth turns clockwise. A clockwise circle has no hard edges and offers no resistance to the great power of life. Circles are smooth, and the absence of edges or squared corners keeps us safe from the feeling that we are nearing the end of something.

If we run into a wall, we are likely to stop, thinking that time contains an end. Such walls call for purification to renew our circular life and thinking. We enter the ceremonial lodge bent down in reverence, humbled before the power of Creation, and crawl in a clockwise direction to the place we will sit. When we leave the lodge, we exit clockwise.

These and other rituals are done with the deepest respect for the oldest living relative we have, the Creator. Virtually every ceremony in our culture honors the Creator and brings into the circle those who serve Him, such as the animals who are His messengers.

The spiral dance

The spiral dance is a metaphor for a variety of ways to see our spirit travel from the earth to the sky to bond with

Creation or the Faraway. The sacred circle always moves clockwise with respect for Creation as its source. We can perform this ceremony in everyday life through the arts, such as in song, dance, basket weaving, pottery making, painting, and various forms of meditation.

Even when we are performing arts that bonds us with Creation, we are in a type of meditation. I remember a coiled basket I once saw, made by Apaches. I noted that the outer design was a clockwise spiral that reached upward to illustrate the meaning of bonding with Creation. The person weaving the basket may have been connecting with the Creator.

I once choreographed a Dance of the Flute to non-Indian music, and when I performed it, the dance took me to the Faraway, or Creation. There is no one way to make contact with the Creator. We can meditate, do breathing exercises, sing, hike to the top of a mountain, or dance in order to become bonded.

We can achieve the spiral dance by weaving dream catchers, or some claim to achieve it through Tai Chi, which they consider a spiral dance. Walking the labyrinth, utilized by many churches, involves physically walking a spiral labyrinth pattern on the ground while meditating. The labyrinth, evident in many religious traditions (the Hopis use it as a pattern in their medicine wheel), is a journey through the spiral dance.

The circular dance pattern can be seen as a mandala, where the personal circle is aligned with the circle of the universe, and so the universal symbol of unity and totality becomes a personal symbol as well.

One of the easiest ways to perform this ceremony is to picture it. We can see ourselves sitting weak upon the ground, and tired from the chores of daily work. Then we may ask the Power of the Universe, the Great Spirit, or whatever name for Creation we choose, to help us stand up tall for the dance. The spiral enables the dancer to center and bring the energies into balance.

For women in Native American traditions, this balance means to connect to the masculine power of Creation through the spiral dance. As women, we also link ourselves to the feminine power of the moon. Grandfather, or the Creator loves to dance, and we are His most desirable partner. To do it in a native way means that we accept the separate powers of women and men.

The core of the spiral dance ceremony is to honor the highest capabilities of ourselves by reaching out to the depth of Creation to bond with it. We are not judged when we seek this bond. Judging is a human concept, not a spiritual one. It is we humans who do all the judging, and not Creation. As we practice union with the greatest Source of our lives, the truth we seek will surely be revealed to us. That truth is about love, compassion, the ability to let go of problems, and rising above the stresses of this life.

Centering through an outdoor meditation

After we seek the bonding, we wait. Now we center ourselves within the grace of gentle silence. We arrange ourselves in a comfortable position, but not so comfortable that we will fall asleep. I simply sit up with my spine straight. I do not cross my legs, but let them rest comfortably. I may focus on something I find spiritually comforting, like the flame of a candle or, if I am outside, the horizon or some benign aspect of nature that is not moving.

We allow the busy mind to slow itself with our eyes open. Relax and breathe deeply and naturally until the metabolism slows down and physical relaxation occurs.

Picture yourself outside yourself dancing a spiral dance. This visualization helps to send away negative thoughts that pass through the mind. Allow them to keep moving and to exit your spiritual circle. They will begin to come less often as you develop the skill of silent meditation.

Some of us may have participated in this ceremony many times, and have become fairly proficient at honoring the silence. For others, it will seem difficult at first, but it's all part of developing our bonding skills. The first time we do this, we may even feel unsuccessful, but we are not. Like any physical muscle, the art and spirituality of contemplation needs to be worked the same as our muscles if we want to develop the dance within us.

We may be aware of distracting physical sensations, such as an itch, or experience difficulty sitting still and breathing slowly. We keep trying, because it is more worthwhile than we can ever imagine. This is the way of our ancestors, but it is uncommon in today's busy lifestyles.

Practice makes us more perfect. The internal ceremony we are practicing has been done in various ways all over the planet for thousands of years by many kinds of people. When we first try this, we only need to do it for a short time. Take only a few moments, and walk your mind through the suggested steps to spiritual visualizations. Do this every day for a while in order to grow and prepare for longer meditations.

Preparation for spiral visualizations

☞ Find a comfortable spot in which to sit.

☞ Relax in the most comfortable position for you.

☞ Focus on a non-moving, pleasing object: a candle, falling water, the horizon, a plant.

☞ Close your eyes and breathe deeply until you
    feel some sense of relaxation.

☞ Visualize a spiral.

☞ If unwanted thoughts enter the spiral, allow
    them to exit on their own, and don't worry
    about them.

☞ Visualize yourself dancing in a spiral.

☞ Visualize yourself bonding with Creation.

☞ Accept whatever comes during this bonding.

Once the desired union with Creation occurs, it becomes a love like no other. The great secrets of life unveil
themselves to us. We receive knowledge, wisdom, and
power from Creation. The experience is unique, personal,
and sacred to each individual. We may only wish to reveal
our personal experiences to a mentor on a like-minded
path. Journaling is another great way to record the feelings
and revelations of the spiral circle to which we journey.

Calling the wisdom

As we continue to practice the spiral dance, and to
develop an intimate trust for the Power of Creation, communication becomes better. We feel the presence of this
power inside us as we move deeper toward Divine Knowledge. We feel grateful and thankful, and may experience
intense emotion as we enter this part of the journey.

If we discover anything negative in the path, we can
ask that it be removed. Then we trust that it will be. As
our trust grows even more, we're aware of going deeper
into the chambers of our consciousness. The presence of
the One to whom we bonded becomes more obvious, and
our fears about the inward journey dissipate.

I have heard people say they believed they were asking
too much of their Creator, but as we journey ever inward,

we are not capable of asking too much if we truly seek this type of bond. Creation is willing to wait until we develop the trust needed to make the journey.

Circle of our belief system

Many books on the exploration of the soul are written by individuals on different spiritual paths. Artists try to paint the journey, and poets write songs and prayers that deal with the supernatural within us. Many try to teach us how to deal with what we encounter on the path of spirituality, including how to break through the blocks and fears that hold us back from this inner journey. These fears, though, are of our own making and cannot really harm us if we deal with them in a sacred way.

Many types of purification ceremonies are performed in an effort to cleanse us of our fears. They are necessary for us to feel safe on our journey. The results are always the same, because the reason for them is the same. We are seekers of safety, security, and comfort, so we don't want uncertain paths.

We can find courage to help us down the path, though, by calling on holy men and women, healers, practitioners, and other helpers whose life purpose is to assist others along the path of spirituality. We can freely ask these spiritually endowed men and women to assist us with their prayers or blessings.

We need them to be nearby, which is okay because they live in every community and small town, no matter how remote. They are natives and others who have truly made the connection we seek, and are willing to help whenever possible. We make a concerted effort to find a good one who is open-minded enough to understand the purpose of our journey. We don't need to necessarily join any group or denomination to get help from these people. We just ask them for a blessing ceremony, and most will be happy to help. If you encounter one of these spiritual contacts who for some reason refuses, turn to another.

When we feel properly purified by their help, we can continue the journey. In time, we begin to find a peace within our circle of spiritual experience that draws us back again and again. Every time we enter into ourselves, we come closer to the center, the heart, the pulse, the true north of all Creation. And we become infused with love, which is our true nature. The experience of following our path and bonding with Creation is impossible to describe from one person to another because we each perceive it from a slightly different perspective. It may take several months, or it may take years to enter into this amazing place, but however long it takes, it becomes the most profound journey we will ever make in this physical life.

My own spiritual journey reached its depth after a Native American "rites of passage." Because it was so incredible, I wish I could hand the journey over to anyone who wants it, but Creation, in His wisdom, wants us to find our own center, or true north.

As we go more deeply into our quest for true north, it's possible to discover places we don't want to go, and we don't have to because we intuitively know when we begin to enter dark areas of the soul. We simply go no farther and ask for spiritual guidance. The Light of Creation leads us away from danger. If we can carry that Light within us, we can face these fears and discomforts well prepared and ready, but no sooner. Sometimes we must step back and wait.

If we are centered, we will know when it is time to move forward into greater self discovery, and when to pull back.

Discovering true north

We can develop an understanding of the sacred circle of Creation and many of the significant places it can occur. A circle has no beginning and no end. We need to find our own individual place to begin our journey, focusing on our true north. We learn the value of some kinds of circles, and the humility needed to function well within that circle.

☞ The family circle pays homage to the elders, and strengthens the bond of knowledge that follows us through life. The family circle, or those from the friendship circle may help us to define our path, and its priorities and boundaries. We can explore the different types of friendship, such as mentors, peers, and those whom we serve if we are mentors. We need to learn to budget our time and resources in such a way that we do not allow ourselves to be drained by those in our circle.

☞ The circle of the body is partly an understanding of how our physical life moves through the cycles of the circulatory and respiratory systems, and also the nervous system. We continually refine the components that nurture us for survival.

☞ The food chain is also a cycle of continuous reproduction of the environment we live in that expresses the amazing circle of the life. The circle of the food chain teaches us that we are as dependent on other animals and life forms as much as they are dependent on us and each other.

☞ The circle of time shows us the unfolding life that begins at daybreak. The separate moons of the year's cycle mark our individual seasons. Everything is marked by these various cycles.

☞ Moving clockwise, as in the spiral dance, is one way we achieve harmony with the natural world. Moving clockwise opens doors into the chamber of ceremony, allowing us to pass through the supernatural realms of consciousness.

☞ The spiral dance ceremony is a commitment to enter into the self on a journey of exploration. The dance provides the necessary tools for a safe journey. The most important tool we need to start the odyssey is centeredness, calling wisdom from the Faraway, and locating someone we trust to help and pray with us as we journey inward and outward simultaneously.

☞ Becoming centered is the act of learning to meditate and to honor the silence. We relax and allow thoughts to pass through us as we breathe deeply. We seek union with the sacred, and it takes a lot of practice and experimentation.

☞ Calling the Wisdom is prayer. It is an invitation to the Great Spirit, or Creator, to enter into our heart and share Himself with us. It is the path to the ultimate mate for our soul and heart. It is not a human power, but rather the other half of our spirit self that longs for union with us.

☞ Nothingness to no-thing-ness is the understanding that, as we begin this journey within, we may think we feel nothing except maybe loneliness or boredom. This is actually the point where we are at the crossroads of transcending the physical world and entering into unfamiliar territory where we soon become aware that the other half of us waits patiently to form a bond that will change us forever.

☞ Our belief system is the supernatural that lives silently within the center of us. Once we achieve true north and find its depth, we are unable to describe it to others. Such description would only serve to dishonor the enlightenment and the sacredness we feel.

3
CREATING YOUR OWN CIRCLE OF POWER

Throughout our lives, we meet people who impress us. Who are they, and where do we know them from? Political, military, or religious histories provide us with knowledge of some of them. They may be heroes who have shaped the thinking of many of their peers, or effectively changed a form of government or spirituality. Some of them become our "knowing ancestors," or mentors, and take their place in our personal circles of power.

Who are the "knowing ancestors"?

India's Mahatma Gandhi (1869–1948), who advocated non-violence to achieve independence from British rule, is an example of philosophies and actions that reflected his spiritual path. He is considered by many throughout the world as one of the greatest heroes of all time. One of his quotes hangs on my office wall where I can see it every time I enter the room. It says, "Be the change you would like to see in the world."

Gandhi's statement is strong. It implies that we need to take responsibility for changing the world around us. This may sound like a tall order for little old us, but if we wish to see change of any kind, we need to contribute something of ourselves to that change.

A few years ago, a TV program about Earth Day featured well-known actors with one thing in common: They asked each of us to take responsibility for our part in saving the environment.

They performed a variety of skits and short dramas about the earth to illustrate the damage humankind has inflicted on this planet. They taught ways to recycle, conserve energy, and cut down on pollution. They used their talents and gifts as actors and performers to tell a dramatic story and offer solutions. Their efforts touched many of the viewing public, which means they did their job well. They did what Gandhi asked of people: become the change you want to see in the world.

As a result of Earth Day, my family began a dramatic recycling project in our home that won us the Recycling Award of the Year from the Big Bear Community Services District. The work of the actors had circled around and touched us in our own small community.

Another group of performers did something similar just days after the September 11 attacks in New York. They contributed their talents for free, asking Americans to pray for peace, band together, forgive, and at the same time, called upon us to take action as a patriotic nation, and be proud to be American.

Both groups of performers, those from Earth Day, and those patriotic ones from the aftermath of September 11 are "knowing" ancestors, because anyone who helps others grow as human beings falls into that category.

"Knowing ancestors" can be historical figures, performers, musicians, artists, authors, or the founders of various spiritual lifestyles. Obviously, they do not have to be from our own family tree, although that, too, is okay. Nor do they have to be perfect. We all need heroes in our lives.

Perhaps we have had a remarkable parent, grandparent, aunt or uncle, or know someone from our spiritual upbringing who displays impressive traits that reflect integrity, honesty, and spirituality.

Some characteristics that produce "knowing ancestors" are:

☞ Humility.

☞ Love of neighbors.

☞ Compassion for those less fortunate.

☞ Joy in a spiritual life.

☞ Contrition.

☞ Purity of spirit.

☞ Courage.

☞ Patience.

☞ Perseverance.

☞ Strong faith.

☞ Love of Creation.

☞ Knowledge and trust in the rightness of things.

Native Americans have a vast record of heroes, some fairly recent, with names known by many, such as Sitting Bull, Cochise, Black Elk, Chief Joseph, Chief Seattle, and Geronimo. Also of note are women, not quite so well known, such as Martha George, an ancestor of Chief Seattle, who founded the Small Tribes Organization of Western Washington with her own money. Sacajawea, a

Shoshone woman, was part of the Lewis and Clarke expedition with her French-Canadian husband, Toussaint Charbonneau.

Many not so notable heroes live or have lived among us. We start to become more aware of them as we read and study their lives in an effort to know how they got the way they did. If we want some of their characteristics, we try to emulate them in our actions—in our circle.

Ascended Masters

Rumors exist of a temple somewhere in Tibet carved from a single piece of ancient stone, possibly marble. The exact location of this temple is unknown. Those who have visited there are not sure about the road or even the elevation. Those who have been lucky enough to accidentally stumble across the temple have been privileged to enter and witness a great mystical experience because it is rumored to be the earthly place of worship for the Ascended Masters of all time.

The Ascended Masters are spiritual prophets and masters of religious history. They derive from what some consider the world's main religions, all of whom possess sacred scripture: Buddhism, Christianity, Islam, Hinduism, Judaism, and Sikhism.

Other paths of spirituality also exist, such as tribal worship found in North and South America, Africa, Australia, and Asia.

The Ascended Masters are spiritual leaders from all of these spiritual groupings, and probably from among the thousands (some estimates place it at 10,000) of other recognized spiritual bodies in the world.

Those who claim to have entered the temple of the Ascended Masters say they recognize some of them, but not all. Some may have lived on earth before recorded history.

If such a place as this Tibetan Temple really exists, wouldn't it be great to be a little mouse in the corner who had the honor of hearing how these Ascended Masters communicate their worship?

Some of the Ascended Masters are believed to have transcended death by rising visibly from the earth to the Faraway. This would express the highest level of spirituality any human has ever achieved. Some people might say these ascended ones were never human. Others would call it mass hysteria or hypnosis. Still others may say the Ascended Masters were actually beings from outer space.

It's not necessary to discern what caused the miracle of ascension to be recorded more times than we are generally aware of throughout the history of the world. At this point, we must decide if we want to believe in miracles or not. If we believe in the supernatural, it's a good chance we might accept the idea, or at least consider that ascension is a possibility.

Once we acknowledge the possibility, we can then begin to seek them as teachers in our medicine circle. If we know of one or more spiritually ascended teacher or master, we can invite them into the circle. It is a native way to seek the highest form of spiritual contact possible, and use every available tool at our disposal that we consider truly sacred. We avoid any contact with dark spirits, who only weaken our circle of power.

Surrounding ourselves with the wisdom of the living

In addition to Ascended Masters—family members who have gone before us, related and unrelated elders, adopted ancestors, and spiritual heroes—we can also count on certain other diverse friends and acquaintances.

I know a holy man who performed the prayers of the ceremony he lead by placing individuals from four distinctly different religions in the four corners of the worship area so the prayers would be balanced. Thus, everyone was served in the circle of prayer. He also invited some very strong spiritual friends to attend, and some elders, all whose presence helped the beginners.

It made for a very special sweet ceremony that included a spiritual invitation from at least one Ascended Master who provided protection from anything evil penetrating the ceremony.

If we want to learn from the world, we can surround ourselves with people who are smarter or more highly evolved than us. They may lose us in conversation once in a while when we don't quite comprehend what they are talking about, but the real lessons often occur when we listen quietly as they talk to one another.

Being in the presence of such worldly and spiritual knowledge is like having a potluck dinner at home, inviting everyone to bring a dish that is peculiar to their culture of origin. We hold such ceremonies in our home several times each year.

Those attending always thank us for inviting them to such a spiritual event, but it's really my husband and I who reap all the goodies. We mix folks from distinct and different backgrounds whom we think are open to native spirituality. We invite a few beginners so they can learn along with us. We sit in a circle and pass an object of power around in a clockwise direction. Everyone who holds the object is asked to share a bit of his or her wisdom with the rest of us. Everyone shares. We do not end the circle until the object has gone all the way around. The more diverse the guests, the better. We have had circles with Buddhist elders, native elders, Reiki healers, priests and ministers, as well as school teachers, electricians, scientists, postal employees, writers, and physicians. It is great to see scientists and holy men share the same sacred circle. We never cease to be amazed at these encounters.

Personal elders

Many years ago, my husband and I made a pilgrimage to the southwest heart of Indian country, 800 miles from our home. We gathered tokens for a sacred ceremony which was to bring our extended family together with the elders and holy people from another tribe. We arrived in this colorful Indian land and settled in for a few days of healing and prayer. As soon as we unpacked, I searched for the oldest man I could find from the tribe. As is customary among Indian people, I offered him a package of tobacco and asked his permission to speak with him.

He said to me, "If someone brings tobacco to the table to ask for the ways, or the language of the old ones, then the tobacco is for the table and not for me." He continued, "I am not the truth. I simply carry the message. Sitting here at the table is the ceremony. I am not really the elder, just the one of the two of us that has more years than the other one, so I may speak. Leave the tobacco on the table where we sit, because the ceremony is now at the table, not because I am here. It is an honor to be sitting at the table where the conversation is about the Greatness of Things."

How wonderful it was to hear this old holy man humble himself before Grandfather in this way, and in his sweet broken English. I knew that I had found the right person to talk to.

A soft afternoon breeze blew around us, bringing relief from the summer heat of the painted desert. A strong spirit of serenity settled over us, and it was as though we were the only two people in existence from our native culture. The breeze moved his gray hair as he spoke slowly with his eyes closed on a face wrinkled and weathered with the knowledge of his years.

"This table is the ceremony where we will learn the old language in our pitiful English. We leave our pain on the table and go back to the now when we leave here. We leave the sad words here at the ceremony. Talk to those lava rocks you have gathered. They are the oldest people who deserve all the respect and care. They heard you and understand because the volcano brought them here to New Mexico before even I was born." We both laughed at his implication of being incredibly old. Sometimes elders repeat things they say for the sake of making a point. I was used to this from my dad, and was prepared to spend how ever many hours it took to listen to everything he was willing to share.

"The rocks are the old ones of the earth. Offer them bits of your food. Offer them everything you have. Talk to them the whole way home in the truck and then listen. Ask the Creator to help you hear their ancientness with the wisdom of the four directions of the wind, so you can learn to speak better in your native language. Understand? Before you build the fire, ask for the strength to do this, and you will not be afraid, because you will have the spirit of the fire in you. But do not disrespect the fire by walking between the fire and the door of the lodge anytime after the fire is burning.

"Keep talking to the fire in a way that no one else can hear, and make offerings of tobacco to the fire. Ask Grandfather to speak the prayers of your language through you and you will remember and understand. Ask for the wisdom of how to show respect for the fire so no one gets burned. Mother, Father, and air are the Creator and the fire is the Great Spirit of the lodge and the stones are the old people and your ancestors. Sing to them so you can be strong and humble."

We stayed and talked until the shadows were long across the timeless desert and it was past the hour for supper. He was the spiritual advisor to help bring together the two tribes that he had never met. He gave his time, a most valuable commodity at his age, to me for free. I took notes furiously all afternoon, filling a spiral notebook. I have used his precious words many times because they hold an encyclopedia of spiritual knowledge.

I also gave tobacco to an old woman at Taos Pueblo on another journey in search of spiritual truth. She too wove a wonderful day full of wisdom and love, wrapped in the teachings of her elders. These people are only a few examples of fine teachers I have been honored to know.

When Dad was 87, the time had come when I knew he wouldn't live much longer. I did not want to have any of that sacred wisdom follow him out of this life unrecorded. I asked him to sit in a comfortable chair in my office, and just talk to me as long as he could. I pecked away at my computer like a mad woman as he spun for me the tales of the travels of our extended family. Through tears of love, I typed everything he said, and arranged those sacred truths of our people into a small book for the generations of us he would leave behind in this modern world.

A few days before he passed over, I sat at his bedside. He could sense my sadness no matter how hard I tried to hide it. He held my hand and told me not to worry, that he would visit my dreams often, and help guide me all my life. He spoke sweetly, and said I would receive all the knowledge I would ever need and much more. I believed him and let him pass to the Faraway in a good native way.

The newfound power of our own circle

The spiritual gifts we receive when we bring knowledgeable and knowing spiritual people into our lives are immeasurable. We honor the quiet time, and learn the arts of the sacred with the wisdom we learn from our meditations, and those who have gone before us.

☞ The knowing ancestors are the heroes of history and the present time who we can relate to as we move through our spiritual life. They can be famous spiritual or political leaders, our own ancestors, performers, writers, artists, philosophers, or other teachers who form new ideas that make sense to us.

☞ Ascended Masters are those who are considered prophets and masters of the mystical world of the supernatural. They can be found in the holy writings of some of the world's current main religions, such as Buddhism, Christianity, Islam, Hinduism, Judaism, and Sikhism. It is said they were able to transcend the power of death by physically rising from the earth to the Faraway.

☞ Some of the positive characteristics we look for in knowing ancestors are humility, love of neighbor and Creation, obedience, and love and joy in their spirituality. Other positive traits are contrition, purity of spirit, courage, patience, perseverance, hope, and knowledge and trust in the rightness of things.

 Surrounding ourselves with the wisdom of the living is an important way to receive feedback as we travel together and help one another to maintain balance, so that we don't get so far out that we are no longer of any earthly good.

 It is good medicine to surround ourselves with people whom we consider to be more highly evolved or more enlightened than we are. We can interact with them ourselves, or watch and listen to them relate to one another in gatherings.

4

THE ROOTS OF NATIVE AMERICAN MEDICINE

The medicine lives in the shadowland. It is found in the long shadows of mesas as they reach across the painted desert, creeping ever further, growing as the sun moves westerly. It is found in the lower reaches of the waterfall, in cavernous coastal beaches, and in the quiet subterranean places of the Plains. This is when the dancers of the spirit appear beneath the contrast of blazing sunlight and the deep cool hiding places of the ancients.

They were here for thousands of years, long before our known ancestors peopled the lands, and before the white man set foot on the sacred soil of our native island.

They whisper the mysteries of healing to those who will listen, but only in severe silence do they reveal the timeless truths to the seeker.

Medicine

Medicine, or healing, which come naturally from the land, and experiences with the native environment are defined differently than traditional Western medicine. Medicine to the Native American has always been holistic, combining spirituality, natural herbal remedies, ceremony, right living, discovery, respect for the earth, and honoring the ancients, elders, and all our relatives. Health, medicine, healing, are all inclusive. They involve our whole lives from the time we arise in the morning, through our dreams at night.

Disease or dis-ease can be defined as a disturbance of the body, mind, and spirit. Organs of the body become dysfunctional. The mind becomes weak, obsessed, addicted, or depressed by dark forces, which do not come from our own rightful place in Creation. The spirit becomes lethargic or atrophied.

The whole person then becomes confused and slothful, unable to perform to his or her fullest potential. Disease is the dark side of our capabilities.

The other side of our capabilities, the true nature of us, is pure, strong, and gifted with many talents, but vulnerable to the fast, competitive lifestyle we know so well in today's society.

Part of this competitive lifestyle causes us to fall under the influence of others, and become lost to our own identity. We can so easily trade the most beautiful parts of ourselves for money, property, and prestige in pursuit of the American dream.

Losing our true identity, though, is not something we need to feel guilty or remorseful about. Rather, once we're aware that our lives are not what we want them to be, it becomes an opportunity to grow. In this life, what we perceive as "problems" can become challenges that serve as touchstones to spiritual growth. They are simply signs along the path of life that thump us on the head to get our attention for some soul searching. Sometimes the ancient ones can help us discover the truths of ourselves. Once we know what is wrong, we can begin the search for solutions, doing whatever it takes to turn the problem (the challenge) into a motivation for change. For instance, a diagnosis of osteoporosis might make a person get up and move about because weight-bearing exercises thwart bone loss.

In the old days, we never questioned getting up and moving about. We did physical work to stay alive. Women, affected in far greater numbers than men by osteoporosis, no longer find it necessary to stay as active as they once did.

Activity among the elderly was enhanced because Native Americans in the past elevated their elders to great status. If they presented an elder with a bundle of sage, it showed they were honoring that person as a spiritual being, instead of an old fart. By elevating that person, if it were a woman, she became an active old woman instead of a retired old crone. Otherwise she died. The old woman, honored by her status, was proud to stay physically active. After all, younger people looked up to her as wise.

So medicine is not simply diagnosing a bad back, or diabetes. It asks what the cause is, and how we can best deal with it.

Medicine is the ability to identify the problem and discover the source of healing for that problem. It becomes not only a time of personal growth, but one of revelation. If we observe ourselves this way, we become excited about our own personal discoveries. New doors open to us through the old medicines.

When a person becomes interested in self-discovery through native ways, the mind is opened to a wonderful journey into the shadowland.

Secrets of the heart

Beyond and beneath all the fast thinking processes and education we receive in this life lies a sacred place. It is in the chains of chromosomes right there in our DNA, the building blocks of life. It is the very soul of our survival as a species. That sacred place is the knowledge of everything supernatural. Natives might call it "secrets of the heart." It may also be called the chakra, the kundilini, chi, or the tabernacle of the soul.

To make friends with this wellspring of living knowledge we need only seek the recesses of our hearts, those deep places where we touch everything else on the planet, natural and spiritual.

This place inside of us is the keeper of our ancient medicines and possesses full and complete understanding of the sacred arts passed down to us from the ancients. It is the place where the order of the entire universe speaks to us, the opening in the ceremonial chamber where the strongest source of life flows through. While we have breath, we have this place.

No matter how confused we may feel from time to time, this sacred place lies there waiting for us to stop and pay attention to our heart of hearts. Discovering this depth is an incredible gift, the gift of life, and the authentic union with the divine forces of natural law.

Finding the heart

Many of us keep the heart locked away deep behind cold steel doors of self discipline and competition with other humans. We do this because we make a conscious decision to try to fit in with the people around us. We seek the approval of others—people pleasing—rather than seeking the secrets of our own spirituality. This behavior renders us powerless as individuals and places us in a position of envy and weakness.

Our heart is hidden away and we are simply copycats. We begin this type of behavior as children who want to interact with others. It doesn't mean we are bad or stupid. It simply implies that we have stunted our own growth and halted the progress of our development. It is natural for children to play copycat.

Rites of passage or the quest

Part of Native Americans' medicine is to reaffirm their continued development at puberty by venturing into the mountains or other places (depending on the part of the country in which they live) that are nature-filled. It is the time to stop the people-pleasing behavior and discover the vision of our lives. Many of the things we thought we learned as small children are revealed as false teachings. For example, if a parent has repeatedly told a child that he or she is stupid or inferior in any way, we discover through the rites of passage at puberty that we have the ability to overcome this falsehood. It isn't something that happens instantly, but the native way provides certain rituals that help the flowering young adult overcome the obstacles of moving from childhood to adulthood.

Sometimes as children we have become conditioned by the adults in our lives to fear spiders, heights, or to embrace other phobic reactions. During the rites of passage, we let go of this type of misinformation from others.

Many native people adopt new names during this initial rite of passage, and even leave behind childhood nicknames they have been given by playmates or adults.

The beauty of this rites of passage is that if we were unable to perform valuable development processes in our youth, we may do it at any time in our lives. The only reason it is usually done at the tender age of puberty among native adolescents is that it helps them decide how to proceed with their education, which will, among other things, determine their adult vocation, calling, lifework, and avocation.

Troubled adults, though, can also turn around their lives by taking part in quests in their later years (see Chapter 9). This renewal at a later age includes Native Americans whose earlier lives led them astray from traditional native ways, and who never received the challenge of the rites of passage.

If we seek the silence of the mountain top, the solitude of ocean waves, the flat Plains covered with grass, we are left to ponder our true selves. We can no longer use the excuse that who we are, or how we behave is someone else's fault.

An added beauty is that we can be comforted in our quest by all of Creation. We find out the true meaning of "alone," and to our delight, discover that it is really an experience of being "one with Creation." We are no longer competing with others. We no longer seek the support of our parents or peers because we make friends with and draw strength and wisdom from the environment in which we have placed ourselves during this quest.

We begin thinking about our immediate tasks—how to survive in our immediate surroundings. We begin learning from the wellspring of knowledge within as it absorbs the strength and wisdom flowing from Creation.

As seekers on our quest, challenge, vision quest, or whatever name it goes by, we become independent thinkers and fully aware of our creative abilities. First, though, we might begin questioning our survival techniques.

☞ How do I protect myself from the cold night?

☞ What will I do if it rains during my time in an isolated area?

☞ What animals might threaten my life?

☞ How will I withstand the darkness?

☞ Will I faint from hunger during my stay?

☞ Do I have what it takes to withstand this for several days?

☞ Will I receive messages, visions, enlightenment?

These are only a few of the questions people might ask themselves during a quest, or rites of passage. But once we tap into those deep recesses of the heart, brought alive by the miracle of Creation, we learn that it isn't so hard to thrive in the world, and we can do it on our own. We don't need help from anyone except Creation, as we alone are able to understand it in our own way. In other words, we learn from within and without at the same time—heartfelt and the great outside.

When this is made evident to us, we become proud of our skills, and feel strong and connected to the Faraway. Many times we laugh at our fears and discover that fear is actually a defect of character rather than a reality.

When we discover during the quest that most of our fears are not a reality, we step into the maturation of our childhood learning. This is where our being all comes together. There is no one to impress. It's okay to cry and snivel a bit, but then get over it and move on.

When the sun rises on the mountain, more often than not, we discover that we have slept, and the morning brings new hope. We are closer to the end of our time on the mountain, and we are still alive.

Perhaps the fears of our childish dependence were unfounded. Perhaps we are stronger than we thought. What a beautiful discovery to see that we are truly survivors after all.

We may be a little weak and hungry at the end of our quest (the time of which can vary), but we now look forward to a hot bath and a warm bed.

Finding the simple, clear way

The thoughts and epiphanies people experience on the mountain are simple in nature. They help us to understand that the finer, more blessed things in life are all quite simple. We become acutely aware that we need never be alone again, even when no other person is around.

We have become united with a power that is far greater than ourselves. It is the gentle order of the spirit on the mountain, or the ocean, or the plains.

It is older than time, as we understand it. It is the Great Master of reality, and we have had the honor of bonding with it.

Joining with other traditions

The experience of joining with the Creation during a quest in no way contradicts other forms of other organized religions.

The founders of many religions had similar experiences in the wilderness. Siddartha (Guatama Buddha) came to grips with the questions and fears of his existence when he found himself under the bodhi (enlightenment tree) out in the wilderness, where he discovered the path to become an Ascended Master.

In the Torah, we can read where Moses discovered the burning bush alone in the mountains. He fought temptation when he spent 40 days in the desert alone in the presence of Satan.

We can see that many prophets of great importance who sought a spiritual experience came, in a sense, "to the mountain." It's doubtful that any of these prophets or saviors would object to their followers seeking the same confirmation of their own beliefs.

Followers of great religions will find that native spirituality strengthens a person's already established faith. Native spirituality can enhance any belief or faith that asks the seeker to examine his or her own motives.

The spirituality of the American Indian does not seek converts. It is not an organized religion, and the various groupings of Native Americans throughout the country see things differently. They honor the Creation in a variety of ways, and don't always agree with one another. But the one thing holds true for all: They honor and turn to Creation for their inner strength and goodness.

Other ways of healing through Creation

Some native people discover what their bodies need by following their dreams or visions. Others seek a well-trained healer who can listen to an individual, observe his or her behavior, and diagnose a problem (most of the time) with alarming accuracy.

The healer's job is to search for an effective remedy that will treat the problem rather than just the symptom. Healing is a rare art, and a good healer is hard to find when it's necessary to look outside ourselves.

Any of us, however, can develop the art of healing ourselves by learning to observe and hear the laws of nature instead of listening to only our symptoms.

When we listen, observe, feel, and hear the laws of nature, we are really stepping into modern science and the discoveries of how the brain works.

Norman Cousins, author of *Anatomy of an Illness*, wrote another book called *Head First*, which has been used by some institutions as a textbook. In it, he describes the activity of the human brain as a control post for millions of messengers who carry instructions to the body's organs without intruding on our consciousness. It's similar to when we blush. Our face is just suddenly bright red, and the first inkling we had of it was when we felt the heat from our face. These messengers of the autonomic nervous system silently tell the body when to react to stress, anger, depression, and many other emotions.

In order to modify physical illness, similar silent messages need to be sent through the centers of the brain to the autonomic nervous system. But it's not as easy as it sounds.

For instance, when our stomach feels as if it is formed into a knot, or our head throbs with pain, the cause is often stress. If we were able, I'm sure most of us would simply tell the brain, "Okay, knock it off. I would really prefer not to experience this pain." Unfortunately, it requires a different tactic.

Pain has been set up as a finely tuned warning system. If there is pain, the body is screaming for attention and most of the time we respond. Unfortunately, too often, we treat that screaming pain with painkillers of one kind or another, which really don't solve the problem.

Instead, we need to pay attention to our whole body and find the root cause. Then we need to treat the challenge holistically, which includes a great deal of realism.

Herbs for the body and practices for the mind

Pretend for a moment that you are a natural healer who suggests herbal remedies and other natural techniques to those who need them. Say that a young mother comes to see you. She has three children under 5 years old. She is on welfare and short of cash, so you have agreed to see her without a fee. She is very thin and pale. The entire time she is discussing her symptoms, she is wringing her hands. Her youngest child is in the infant seat at her feet. He is cutting teeth, so he is whining and appears agitated. She sits with her knees tightly pressed together. She is leaning forward with her spine rounded tightly. She does not look you in the eye, but stares at the floor as she speaks. Her nails are bitten down to the quick. As she talks, she puts her hand on her stomach and rubs back and forth to indicate where it hurts. She tells me her doctor said her stomach hurts because of stress.

Even if you were completely unable to understand a single word she said, you would pretty much get the picture. She is nervous, and it's apparent that she seems to feel overwhelmed by her demanding family, but she is loyal to them and takes her kids wherever she goes. So you talk to her about what's going on in her life, without planting any ideas or observations of your own. Does she ever get a break from caring for the children? Does she have time to sit down and eat a regular meal? Does she feel more nervous than usual?

You think about the herbs you could prescribe to rid her of some of the pain. This way, you could quickly get rid of her. But would you really be helping? Or maybe you could suggest that she get a stroller for her infant so she wouldn't have to carry his weight on her back. You might also suggest some yoga exercises for her posture, and some relaxing Chamomile tea for her nerves.

What about a daily walk for her and the kids in a natural setting where they can spend quality time together and smell the flowers? Does she dance with her kids? Finger paint with them? These activities are creative, and have been shown to reduce the risk of several diseases. Is she aware that a couple of minutes of good belly laughter can eliminate pain for a couple of hours?

The point is, if we want to change what goes on inside our bodies, we have to change what goes on outside them. Native peoples have known this for thousands of years, but like the rest of the world, until recently, it wasn't equated with the midbrain. We just knew that we had to react outside, in order to heal inside.

If we can learn to evaluate ourselves as well as we have evaluated this welfare mother, we can learn to let go of most of the pain, and often all of the other physical problems from which we suffer.

We communicate with the midbrain through action! Behavior, sometimes even oddball behavior, truly changes our health for the better. Stories exist about native healings involving people riding their horses backwards, washing themselves with dirt, and drying themselves with water. Sound weird? Of course it does, but the stories are true examples of extreme behavior modifications that can help a person to heal.

Modifying daily habits for health

Many of the daily habits we practice are unnecessary. We develop them in the first place so that we can save time and get organized. Sometimes we place far too much importance on time and organization. If we are not careful, we can organize ourselves right into the hospital, or worse, into a mental ward.

As we move toward a spiritual way of dealing with our everyday life, we can open ourselves to a more supernatural way of doing some things that may have become routine, even boring.

One Buddhist observance for daily living is to once in a while alter the chair we usually sit in for breakfast, or maybe sit on the floor relaxing on a bunch of pillows to watch TV instead of the comfy, plush chair. Changing a usual routine promotes a new perspective of the universe. It helps to make us more creative.

The universe is filled with solutions to boredom, sickness, poverty, and all other sufferings of the human spirit. We need only stop focusing on the habitual behavior of day-to-day living, and take on a wider understanding of the universe swirling about us.

- ☞ What is really out there in the vastness of the great sky?
- ☞ What awaits me on a mountain trail, or in my own backyard?
- ☞ How does the weather feel on my skin today?
- ☞ Does the house smell differently since I cooked breakfast?
- ☞ Can I try a different route to work, maybe veering from the freeway even though it takes a little longer?
- ☞ Why not jump in that puddle over there?

How we can heal ourselves and others the native way?

As children, my grandmother used to take us for walks in the mountains where she pointed out herbs used for remedies that grew on the slopes. When a child is trained this way, as adults we find ourselves looking around in familiar environments to see if we can find some of the trappings of our childhood.

While out walking I might look for a large granite rock near a mountain trail, or a Yerba Santa growing nearby. Nothing in the wilderness has really changed that much since Grandma was alive, although I live in a different part of the country. Smoked Yerba Santa can still be used to treat an asthma attack, and Yerba Santa tea also made a fine remedy for flu symptoms if a person could stand the taste.

As the warm spring brought blooms to every green leafed herb, tiny feverfew daisies would sprout in a whiskey barrel in the front yard. Grandma used the delicate flowers in tea to cure migraines and also to expel mucous if someone had a chest cold. If one of us had a bad dream, she would sit with us and listen to the details while we sipped Chamomile tea until we were drowsy enough to return to bed.

Part of the healing was the way she listened, no matter what you told her. She always reacted with sympathy and compassion. So it isn't just the treatment that heals, it's the hands-on understanding and caring that sometimes makes the medicine do its work. In truth, the caring and attention are part of the medicine.

What has changed today is that we don't take the time and patience to observe, to listen to others and to care, which is all part of our healing and medicine—theirs and ours.

The healing art of observing and listening

One way of learning about the power of observing and listening is with the talking stick, which can be used in any number of settings.

We use a talking stick during some of the meetings we have in our home. The talking stick is part of our "talking circles" where everyone in the circle gets a chance to share (see Chapter 7).

The person holding the talking stick (sometimes called a prayer stick) has the right to speak and the right to be listened to. While the person holds the stick, no one else can interrupt or throw in his or her two cents. Everyone else in the circle has nothing to do but listen and pay attention to the person talking.

In our usual everyday discourse, it is rare that we get to speak a complete thought without being interrupted. Often, we don't truly listen because we are so busy thinking of what we are going to interject as soon as we get the chance. We don't fully hear the person who is presently speaking because we are concerned with our own opinions.

One woman who had never participated in a talking circle previously said it was one of the most exhilarating experiences she'd ever had—to be truly and deeply listened to.

Actually, I have never met anyone who didn't enjoy the talking circle. We all learn from one another, and in the listening, we heal.

During some talking circles, we may begin with a blessing, purification, or by honoring the Creator, but it isn't always necessary to perform a ceremony to show the courtesy of truly listening to another. It is all good medicine.

Meditating the native way

The purpose of meditation is to empty the mind, and when we do, we are well on the way to spiritual healing.

Many ways of meditating exist, arriving from a variety of disciplines and different faiths. No one way is the perfect way.

One woman I know uses walking as her meditation. It centers her. She has even written a book about it. She not only interacts with Creation during her walks, but she is taking action for her health. Her midbrain is active while she is meditating.

Another man, an American Indian from a local tribe, suffered from alcoholism and illegal drug addiction for many years. Finally he entered a 12-step recovery program and enjoys being clean and sober today. When he first began recovery, he discovered that he had many emotional trials to endure, as most do in recovery. He began running, and worked himself up to 26 miles around the reservation every day. He worked out his frustrations and made a conscious contact with Creation as he ran. He reached a higher plane of consciousness through his physical action. Running helped him tap into the subconscious.

When he first sobered up, he looked angry and withdrawn. He was a quiet man with a mild stutter. He dressed like a tough guy and wore his short black hair slicked back. After a year into recovery and several hundred miles of running, his entire appearance changed for the better. Then he began to spend time with the elders and started following the traditional ways of his people.

Now he wears his hair in a long tail down his back and sings with the bird singers of the tribe. He runs sweat lodges and councils youths who suffer from drug and alcohol abuse. As the years passed, he became a holy man for his people. He is soft spoken, with every word well chosen. The stutter is completely gone.

The point is, just entering into a 12-step program might have solved his problems with drinking and drugs, but did not bring him as close to the Creator. It took both the program and the running, which is a form of meditation (or focus) for him to reach his highest potential and heal himself.

Meditation is that powerful, and teaches us to focus on the greatest power available to us.

Some people find that meditation works best when they sit as motionless as possible and practice deep breathing exercises. This clears the mind and relaxes the whole body. Others find it useful to focus on some kind of religious icon or drumming. Some chant mantras. Some use different scents, music, a burning fire, or even a candle.

Surrendering to the spirit

A true surrender of the whole self to a greater spirit is not an easy thing to achieve. We spend a huge part of our lives controlling and managing everything around us. Therefore, to surrender our will and lives is very foreign and feels almost unnatural. Even if we are normally very passive, we manipulate our environment by allowing others to control the activities around us.

As we take the posture of a follower, we are still controlling our place in society. We have just allowed others to control it for us. Every form of action and communication is the result of a conscious decision that affects the outcome of our choices.

In order to achieve peace among the tribes, we lay down all weapons of the body, mind, and spirit. Warfare ends and we surrender our defense to one another. When we sweat on someone else's reservation, we do it their way, which can be very different than the way we were taught in our own tribes or extended families.

To borrow from the white man, "When in Rome, do as the Romans." We do not offer a song unless we are invited to do so. We honor the spiritual leader with a small gift and express humility and gratitude that we are honored by the invitation to join their people in worship. We then make every effort to follow and learn quietly whatever they choose to teach. We do not challenge a holy man, no matter how much we think we already know about the ceremony.

We are visitors who have come to honor our Creator by acts of generosity and respect. If the ceremony is for some reason distasteful to us, or we become frightened, it is acceptable to wait for the proper moment and excuse ourselves quietly.

We are always grateful to have been invited and express this at the beginning and the end of any ceremony or ritual. We never interrupt during a prayer or during the silence. Native people remain reserved in opinion and action when we are new to someone else's land. We do not express our opinion until we are asked, and even then are very careful to remain as detached as possible.

This is not an act of arrogance or unfriendliness, but rather an act of sacred respect for all living things, as embodied by our hosts.

If we have come in contact with our spiritual lives to any degree or depth then we are sure of ourselves and feel well protected by our own concept of Creation at all times. Even when things get a little strange during someone else's ceremony (which they do many times), we keep to ourselves and are silent with our personal prayer and protection.

Being able to abstain from infringing on a host's beliefs and rituals is a sign of personal strength and courage that comes with our individual spiritual path. There is always something to be learned from any experience we encounter. Sometimes we learn what we don't want to learn from others. But these lessons are just as valuable as the ones that enlighten us. Sometimes a host may have made a poor impression on me and I learned not to do those types of things when I invite others to my domain.

We are never better than an apology if it becomes necessary, but no one is asked to crawl before any other. We simply make our amends clearly and let it go with a humble attitude. This is the proper way of things. Our connection with Creation will never let us down. We can only better ourselves by showing respect for others. This is true dignity.

The medicines of the people of our first nations are very old and powerful, like the fire that burns the forest to clear the land. Miracles happen constantly and visions and profound changes in reality are common in ceremony. We accept this and understand that our truth may be different from someone else's.

When we join in ancient ceremony of any kind, we understand that we are praying for an experience involving the supernatural, so why would we act shocked when it happens and our prayers, or someone else's prayers, are answered? Also, we have no way of knowing what kind of spiritual path a stranger in the group may practice, so we always remain ready and prepared for anything. If we truly trust our own Creator and the things we have been taught, then there is nothing to fear.

We may witness amazing cures, or seemingly hopeless states of the body, mind, or spirit in others or in ourselves. Spirituality and wisdom are the most worthy of all the journeys we can take in this life. We will not regret any meeting of the human form with Creation if we become spiritually fit before embarking on this sacred red road of mystery and incredible discovery.

The red road to Native American medicine

The red road is the path of Native American spirituality and its healing medicine. It is a general intertribal term that means the difference between a road or path of light and discovery, rather than one of darkness.

☞ Native American medicine is understanding and bringing healing and enlightenment to the human experience as we develop an understanding of self and the power of Creation. All healing begins with spiritual understanding.

☞ The secrets of the heart are those wonderful gifts we are born with that live in our DNA, and are available to us whenever we need them. Everything we ever want to know about the wisdom of the ancients is already in our hearts. We are truly more spiritual than physical, and it is our quest to come into union with this internal wisdom.

☞ The midbrain is the place where spiritual change has its effects on the human body. As we transfer our physical experiences and disciplines into behavior, we become healed at the physical level. In other words, the way we use our voluntary nervous system has long-term effects on the autonomic nervous system or the involuntary system of the body.

☞ Herbs can many times be used in the practice of physical or psychological healing, but we seek to treat the real problem rather than the physical symptoms. We avoid painkillers as much as possible because pain is an alarm telling us to pay attention so that we may discover the actual cause of our suffering. Perhaps the pain has absolutely nothing to do with the physical body.

☞ Practices for the mind call us to stretch our mental muscles to higher places of the eternal spirit of Creation. Use of tools such as meditation or physical activity and instruments of focus. Incense, music, fire, or religious icons are helpful in developing the focus of an otherwise busy mind.

☞ Surrendering to the spirit of Creation is essential in any type of ceremony. We begin this process by showing extreme respect and dignified reserve for the individual who is the celebrant or holy man. We honor his land and his ways no matter how unfamiliar they may appear at first, but we reserve the right to respectfully exit if we are uncomfortable with any ritual. We do not compromise our own rights nor do we infringe on the rights of others. We always trust our own teachings and gut feelings to carry us through, and to help us achieve either protection or enlightenment, whichever is available to us.

5

GATHERING PERSONAL MEDICINE

Gathering personal medicine is a life's work that begins at birth. It means more than collecting "stuff" or "tokens," especially for certain types of bundles. Yet, other types of bundles we need to discard. Personal medicine is not as confusing as it might sound, but it follows us every minute of the day throughout our journey on the red path.

Budgeting time

I have just come out of my mother's womb and into the world. I was not prepared for this. The world is huge, noisy, cold and oh, my Creator, I am naked!

How do I live with this new knowledge that is slamming into my mind, body, and soul at speeds so fast that I cannot fathom it all at once? What am I supposed to do with this brand new tiny naked body, and a life expectancy in my country of birth of over 70 years? How will I handle my time?

Part of Native American medicine involves budgeting time and finding peace for those bedeviled by the type of time we encounter in this world.

What is the most important thing that you, as an individual, do every day? Some will contend it involves their job or vocation. Others believe it is their children who hold first priority. To some, it may be a lover. For many others, spirituality is the top priority of the day. Along with these, we also deal with the usual food preparation, driving to and from work, paying bills, tending to sick children, illness among friends and family, gatherings, house cleaning, taking children to extracurricular activities, and a multitude of other chores.

These are important priorities that need attending. It is my belief, and that of many other native people, that by making certain to attend to our spirituality, and the well being of our minds and bodies, that day-to-day living will go much smoother. Practicing Native Americans can be said to fulfill their spirituality from the time they arise in the morning and throughout their sleep at night because their dreams continue the daily life cycle.

Included in the budget for our usual work day, we need to set aside minutes or hours for exercise, spiritual devotion, leisure, and creative endeavors. Before we decide how to balance these activities, though, we need to discern our greatest needs.

Putting first things first

When we come into this world, most of us are equipped with certain instincts that enable us to live productively throughout our lives. An instinct is a natural or inherent aptitude, impulse, capacity, or tendency that is unalterable in humans (and other organisms as well). It does not involve reason, but is an unconscious response to our environment. Instincts are driven by something greater than us—our Creator.

The instinct for survival, when it responds to a threat, becomes a fighter because the instinct is far more powerful than the desire to be nice to others. We all know people in our lives who always appear angry, or in a constant state of conflict. Perhaps they feel their very survival is somehow threatened. The actual threat may have occurred a very long time ago, but it may have been so incredibly frightening that the instinct for survival has taken over, causing the person to be in a state of perpetual anger.

To procreate is another powerful and obvious instinct. Yet, it too is another drive that can be corrupted by some traumatic event that lasts a lifetime.

On another level, we are also guided by certain basic human needs, such as food, clothing, and shelter. To meet these needs, we labor and acquire goods. We often become unhappy when these basic needs aren't met. Once met, though, we can rest and relax, but sometimes that also takes work or maintenance. For example, all human relationships take work. If we want a relationship with a mate to bear love and fulfillment, it requires work. The same applies to relationships with children, other family members, and friends.

Our relationship with the Grandfather of us all also requires time and work. It would be very selfish to simply present the Creator with a list of needs and expect immediate gratification. We wouldn't want anyone to treat us that way, so why should we expect it to be okay to treat the Grandfather in such a way?

It is nice when we are told by someone, "I love you," and to have others do nice things for us or give us gifts. Native people make many offerings to the Creator, such as burning sweet grass, sage, or other herbs we believe He likes to smell. We also make offerings to the Mother Earth, because she is next in line of our providers—not second, but next.

The reason the Creator comes first is because our relationship with Him is forever, and the place we stand on the earth, represented by Mother Earth, is only temporary. We offer first to our permanent companion.

If we attend any ceremony on a reservation, we see a great expression of gratitude offered to Grandfather before anything else is done. It has always been this way, and it is hoped of those who honor the old ways that it will be kept alive. That is because through the eons, we have learned that when we place our spirituality first, everything else falls into place.

Medicine bundle tokens

Tokens are anything from rocks and feathers to diamonds and gold, and everything in between. They are simply objects that hold special meaning to us as individuals. To a Buddhist, a lotus flower may be a token; an Eagle feather may serve a Native American; and to a Catholic, a crucifix or rosary. Tokens have nothing to do with monetary value. People gather tokens that represent their spiritual path, and they become part of our personal medicine.

Some people carry their tokens in a small leather bag around their neck. This bag may contain several very small objects from nature. The reason for gathering tokens is to have a collection of things very personal to our own individual spirituality. No two people will carry the same exact tokens. Sometimes they are small things given to us by someone we love very much. They can be something picked up from the ground at mountain tops where we may have bonded with the Creator. It may be a brightly colored rock or shell from a beach where we experienced a romantic walk with someone special. It could be a deceased grandmother's wedding ring, or a wilted flower given us by our firstborn when he or she was a toddler. It is anything that represents love, spirituality, culture, or anything with a strong positive effect on us.

We may spend a year gathering these things, and keep them in a little box until we feel that everything we need to create our personal medicine bundle has been gathered. Then we spread them out, and look at them to remind us of the sacredness of each one and the special value it holds for us. We touch them, and relive the reason we collected them in the first place. They may not look like much, but they are actually objects of healing for us.

Anything that makes us feel love and spirituality has a positive effect on the autoimmune system. For one thing, the objects make us reminisce, which has been shown to be healthful for, not only old people, but the young as well.

It isn't that early Native Americans understood the science behind today's studies showing that reminiscing, being positive and optimistic, feeling loved, laughter, and other emotions keep the immune system strong. Through observation, they simply knew it worked.

Because life is tough, it's important to continually boost our morale, our attitudes. The medicine bundle, holding memories of things that bring us joy, is one of those touchstones, one of those icons. When we are near those icons, we feel safe, loved, and relaxed. They are health giving, and they have nothing to do with anyone else's spirituality but ours.

Once we have gathered the very powerful medicine to help carry us through the tough times, we need to prepare a special package for them, just large enough to carry them, but small enough so that they aren't particularly noticeable to others. It needs to be durable and lightweight. Leather has been used for personal bundles through the generations by natives.

The blessing ceremony

Once the bundle is prepared, it needs to be offered to the Creator for purification. We can simply hold it up high outdoors as though the mystery of the Great Sky would take it in His hands and bless it for us. Pray in your own way that the Creator do this. Stand silent for a few minutes. Trust that this blessing has occurred, and give thanks as you hold it near your heart. This act of faith seals the medicine within the bundle. Now it belongs to you to share with Creation.

Now, it is as though when we hold the bundle and pray to the Creator that the bundle is a form of identification with ourselves and the awesomeness of the union with Creation. It combines the selected objects with the love you felt from the Creator.

Purification of the bundle is known as ritualistic prayer, which means that it was done almost exactly the same as it has been done for centuries. Ritualistic prayer is simple ceremony, and the Greatness of Things loves it that way.

The burden bundle

The burden bundle represents our lack of willingness to accept our spiritual path. It is filled with ideas that separate us from our own concept of Creation. A life fueled by self will and lack of acceptance for the Greatness of Things lacks meaning. To a Native American, it is the extreme state of powerlessness. It is our dark side, and we need to acknowledge this dark side of ourselves in order to enjoy the treasures of Creation.

When we acknowledge the dark side we are able to crawl into the sweat lodge as an act of physical submission to Creation. Submission is a great and powerful act of humility. It is so filled with surrender that it becomes the very essence of the true path of medicine.

The Sundance may epitomize the greatest act of humility. Because it is so very sacred to our people, and even though many know of its components, I am not permitted to describe it verbally or in writing. But one important aspect of the ceremony is the sacrifice of self to Creation for the good of our earthly brothers and sisters. If those who practice the Sundance were not completely submerged in this surrender and bonded with the Grandfather, they would be unable to physically withstand the rigors of the Sundance. The Sundancers are the most respected holy ones in all of Indian County. They have dared to step beyond the majority of us in the execution of their beliefs. They have acknowledged their dark side, and submitted to the deepest form of humility.

How to gather the burden bundle

The dark side of us cannot be ignored, even though most of us do not perform the Sundance. Another ceremony, however, acknowledges the dark side, and allows us to change the things we can. For if we deny that side of us that is filled with ego and separation from the sacred, then the path of the American Indian is useless. Absolutely every aspect of the life of a person with "medicine" is shot through with the thread of Creation, good or bad.

The purpose of the ceremony of the burden bundle is to turn poison to medicine. To perform this ceremony, we gather up some stones. They may be a few inches long or high, so that they are large enough to write on or paint. We gather some small ones and some larger ones, and some that are so heavy we can barely carry them. There may even be some we cannot lift alone. The largest stones are the most effective, but we don't gather them if we are not willing to make huge changes in ourselves. These are reserved for changes that require help from others.

The really huge stones represent the things in our lives that are our greatest troubles, such as life-threatening addictions to alcohol or drugs, or to relationships that we feel locked into that can actually cause us harm, physically, mentally, or spiritually.

These huge stones can also represent horrendous health problems such as cancer, AIDS, and other afflictions. We decide for ourselves what size each stone needs to be in order to represent its respective problem.

We gather this mix of stones because along with our largest difficulties are many smaller ones. We choose the stones very carefully as we gather them. The best stones are gathered from unspoiled areas as close to absolute wilderness as possible.

Each stone is chosen with the "burden" or particular problem in mind. We choose beautiful stones, because our burdens are beautiful if they are used in a good way.

The poison for us are the debts we hold against others, the resentments and lack of forgiveness to others for crimes against us, real or imagined. These things are the seemingly small stones, but when we keep them all together in one place, they become the great boulders and precipices that threaten a deadly fall into the great unknown. Small stones can bond to becomes mountains that despoil Mother Earth.

So while we may think of the really large burdens in our lives as our biggest problems, we begin to understand they are really made of all the smaller characteristics of our lives. This means that the small stones are really the most important ones to gather for the sacred giveaway.

It's okay to acknowledge the huge boulders, but before we break our backs carrying them to the car, we might do better to begin with a larger bundle of the smaller stones. If we do that, we might not need to return with a tractor for the boulders after all.

How to use the burden bundle

We begin another path of self-discovery when we take the burdens home. Every time we enter into an awareness of a negative or dark part of ourselves, we select a stone to match it in size and beauty. We hold the stone and pray for Grandfather to help us change. Then we decorate the stone with colored chalk, paint, crayons, or whatever we can to enhance the rock, and make it our own personalized burden.

Write a one-word description of the burden on the stone. Only one succinct word is allowed, in order to keep it very simple.

Comparative studies of the world's main religions show that each one has accepted descriptions of the worst defects of our human character. And each provides words to describe those defects. It illustrates that every well-known spiritual path gives considerable weight to understanding the darkest areas of our nature, and providing ways of dealing with them.

Some of the darkest areas of our nature include:

- Pride—a reflection of arrogance, self-importance and conceit.
- Greed—unstable desire for possessions and pleasures.
- Lust—ycarning and hunger to an extreme.
- Anger—fury, rage, annoyance at things inside and outside us.
- Envy—resentment of what others possess.
- Gluttony—excess in food, sex, material wealth.

☞ Sloth—laziness and inactivity.

☞ Selfishness—the opposite of our sacred giveaway.

☞ Dishonesty—untruthfulness with others as well as ourselves.

☞ Fear—which paralyzes us to right action.

All of these defects (and others you might think of) are the types of words to be written on these smaller stones that we have gathered, but only if we are truly convinced of their existence within us. Once marked, we put it among the others in the burden bundle. We can keep them in a basket, bag, or any type of container. Just keep them together.

The burden bundle is just as sacred as any other medicine bundle, because at the conclusion of this ceremony, we enter an area of freedom.

Sacred pilgrimages for the burden bundle

As we enter the freedom wrought by the burden bundle when the ceremony is done effectively, we might want to keep it going forever. We begin to realize that all of us spend our lives gathering burdens and ridding ourselves of them, if we are to grow spiritually at all.

The first sacred pilgrimage we make is to complete the ceremony of the burden bundle. Again, we go as far into the wilderness as possible. We can even go to the same place where we collected the stones. But if possible, we go farther. We are going to change the natural arrangement of nature, and in turn it will change us.

We carry our bundle within our arms in a bag that is easy to carry. We walk as far as we feel is necessary in the service of bonding with Creation. How far we walk is linked with the time we budget for spirituality in our lives, and how much effort we are willing to invest. But we must walk. We place our rocks and stones at various places in the wilderness with care and a prayer to Creation.

By now we are very much aware of the character defect that we are ridding ourselves of, and leaving behind. By helping others, and with the help of the Greatness of All Things, they will stay in the wilderness.

A youth and his burden

One time I was asked to do a continuing lecture series for a youth group staying in a beautiful mountain camp near the San Gorgonio wilderness in California. They were placed there for drug rehabilitation. We took the young teens on this journey with their burdens. They all carried their armload of rocks as we hiked to our destination. Some of the kids were at the camp pretty much against their will. Some the courts had placed, and others were brought by concerned parents. About half were there voluntarily. One boy, small for his age, whom I'll call Billy, had no interest at all in what we were doing. But his journey, laced with defiance, turned into a good one.

He knew reports would be submitted to his probation office about his performance, so he went along, but did as little as possible with a very negative attitude. The others didn't much care for him. He didn't fit in with them, and had given up trying. I instructed the group to walk as far as their desire to solve their problem led them. Billy walked about three steps and dumped his poorly painted efforts on the ground in front of him. The rest of the kids began laughing and making fun of him.

I distracted them by saying they needed to place their burdens carefully on the mountain, because the way they affected the environment could last a lifetime. I added that if they truly liked themselves, they would contemplate their actions while they placed their stones. Billy promptly began throwing his rocks in every direction, causing the others to duck and run. His actions didn't surprise me. Experience on my own path has taught me about those of us who carry extra heavy burdens in life. Billy had endured a very rough childhood, one that had stolen his birthright of joy and spirituality.

When he completed his tantrum, I walked over and placed my hands on his shoulder. I told the group that Billy had done the best he could, and that if the others were going to judge him, they needed to look for another stone to add to their collection, and to decorate it in honor of their own defect of judging. It would become their newest and greatest burden. Then I said they could all do as they pleased while I gathered my own stones to distribute on the mountain.

They didn't quite know what to make of my actions, so they waited and watched as I gathered my own burdens. Additionally, I had hidden a large stone in the trunk of my car before we left that morning.

Now I opened the trunk and put my arms around the huge, heavy, dirty rock. I grunted and groaned as I tried to lift it, but the stone was too great, and it remained in the trunk. I was wearing a white blouse and turned to face the kids with dirt all over my body. I walked among them and told them what the heavy rock meant to me.

"I am just a dumb Indian," I said. "I can't help you. I cannot even pick up this stupid rock, and I forgot to paint it. I'm not a psychiatrist or doctor or anything. I don't know why they asked me to come talk to you guys. I had problems when I was your age, and I hated my life."

I continued and began to weep as I spoke to them. "You are all very beautiful in the eyes of your Creator. I cannot convince you of that. Who am I? Just a silly woman, but your Creator knows your heart. You are stuck here with me, but do something for yourselves. I don't care what, but just have the courage to let Him change you, right now! Just ask. I dare you!" I returned to the car and began wrestling with the dirty rock that had not been painted.

Billy came up behind me. His heart had gone out to me. He said the magic words: "Lady, let me help you. You know you are making a fool of yourself." He grabbed the other end of the dirty rock and together we carried it into the woods, and set it down while the others followed. I thanked him, and we embraced.

"Look what happened to Billy," I said. "When he was of service to someone who looked more foolish than anyone, he was healed for the entire duration of his service to me, from the pain of his own burdens. How can helping others help us? Can we help each other carry our burdens? What do you think? You guys are in charge of the rest of this pilgrimage. What do we do now?"

Sharing the light

The kids spent the next few hours helping one another carry rocks to various places in the forest. Everywhere we went was different than the last. They began to lose track of which burdens were their own as they served one another. We put some beautifully decorated stones in amazing places. Some were placed in rivers with our prayers that if we changed the course of the river, the change would bear the marks of our love for Creation. Each kid chose a different place at the end of a silent walk to mark the end of his or her chosen path, and all the others followed. Each person was instructed to pray out loud in his or her own way, naming the Creator by the name they liked best. The journey was a miracle beyond my wildest expectations. The blessing that I received was the ability to cry and become needy when it was necessary to lead my little group of 12 "troubled teens" through the woods in the "Indian way," the most natural way available.

Sometimes, our emotions play an important part in sharing the truth, as we know it, with others. Earlier on the morning of the trek with the teens, I had stopped on my drive to the camp because I felt compelled to pull over to pick up a dirty rock.

Completing my drive to camp, I became very excited and had to watch the speed at which I drove. I could hardly wait to get here, because I sensed something magical was going to happen with those kids. When I was asked to work with the kids, it had seemed an awesome gift, so I surrendered to the Great Spirit as I prayed and drove through the entrance of the camp.

Pilgrimages designed to bond with our Creator are the best experiences we can have if we are willing to place our trust in the Maker of us.

The home is also a place of healing

The most sacred place of all within the circle of life is our home. Just like the circle, there should be no "sharp edges." Teepees, hogans, and wikiups were round with no dark corners to clean, but their roundness isn't all that we mean by "sharp edges." Sharp edges are anything that makes us frown or feel bad when we come in contact with it through any of our senses. Dark corners are those places where things are hidden and made useless by their hiding places. They are like the dead, and carry only weight within them. They need to be recycled. Holding onto useless objects is like living in the past.

Medicine ways

We gather medicine to ensure a safe and spiritual journey on the red path. The ways of medicine involve every phase of our lives—work, home, leisure, exercise, giving, and relationships. A great deal of medicine that is needed to protect us from the rigors of daily living involves natural instincts. Most importantly, healthful survival involves a relationship with Creation.

☞ Budgeting time establishes how we stay on a path that takes us to our desired destination, so that no conflicts are created among the many demands of life.

☞ Tokens for the bundle are items of a person's own choosing that remind them of a loving experience that makes them feel good about themselves. These small items lift our spirits when we see them, and provide strength, healing, and enlightenment.

☞ Once we have gathered the tokens, before we place them in a bag or bundle, they need to be blessed, either by someone else, or we can do it ourselves in a ritual offering to the Creator. This is the time we begin to share ourselves and everything we are about with the greatest Power of all.

☞ Another important ceremony is the burden bundle, which expresses the dark side of our true nature. As we move through the life of the burden bundle, we see the need to let go of our limitations and discover ways to serve one another.

☞ Sacred pilgrimages are journeys we take for the purpose of learning more about our relationship with Creation. Sometimes we need to go somewhere new with a joyful attitude and an open mind. It is an offering we make in trade for spiritual knowledge. We take things as they come and try not to manipulate the outcome with our own self-will.

☞ We share the light to open the sacred heart of us with the absolute trust that it is the right thing to do. We never know who can learn from this act, so we just wait and see. The act could be for our own learning or someone else's or both. Our feelings begin to dictate how we act and we are confident that the Master of our sacred destiny knows how to direct everything in the circle that we travel within.

☞ The home is a place of healing, we need to create a loving, spiritual, and restful environment. It helps to rid the home of burdens— objects that no longer serve a purpose and are hidden in corners.

6

Calling Wisdom From the 7 Directions

All parts of ourselves, the earth, and the Faraway are included when we honor the seven directions. Of the 700 tribes in the United States, I have no right to give honor to any one of them more than others, because I am of mixed lineage. The beliefs, rituals, ceremonies, and customs of all tribes vary slightly, so the information on the seven directions is considered intertribal. In addition to the directions, and the seasons for which they stand, the directions also include the four colors of humankind, red (east), yellow (south), black (west), and white (north).

Sacred beginning: the east

The sun rises in the east, the place of sacred beginnings. The color of this direction is red, according to those who taught me. Some people who build the lodges for sacred ceremonies build them with the door facing east to honor the beginning of Creation, and therefore, the beginning of prayer. We begin the offering of ourselves in the direction of sunrise.

Sacred objects to be used in the ceremony, such as Eagle feathers, Bear claws, a sacred pipe, or other icons that have special meaning and have been blessed, are held up to the sky in the eastern direction. We give thanks to east for the start of Mother Earth. We thank east for the light of day that brings color to the world. We observe east for the location of the sun, showing us what time of the year it is. The time of east is spring.

We thank the direction for the Creation stories that teach our people how to pray and how to understand the Grandfather. The red of east also is the color of our blood, the very life of us. Red is the color of beginning, living, passion, and death because in the circle, the beginning touches the end. The beginning is part of the end.

Eagle comes from the east

My teachers say that Eagle comes from the east, and she is the most sacred of birds because in our country, she flies higher than all other birds. When she is flying so high, she can look down on us from above and we look very small. She sees us with objective and clear eyes. Her perspective is unlike ours because her view is much broader. She watches over us, and is able to scrutinize our every move and thought. This information she takes to the Grandfather. She is a channel from us to Him. She also carries our dreams to the Faraway.

When Eagle circles, which she loves to do, she turns her body sideways so that one wing faces up, and the other faces Mother Earth. She connects our Mother Earth and Father Sky as our parents. When her wings touch the Great Spirit, she is blessed more than anything we can imagine. We are too far from the sky to physically touch Him as Great Eagle does, so if she makes us the gift of one of her blessed wing feathers, we become blessed too.

When we hold Eagle's wing feather toward the eastern sky, standing before our Creator, we realize our greatest power as native people, say the elders who taught me.

If Eagle gives us a tail feather, she gives the gift of sacred direction in our lives. The tail is the rudder of the body of Eagle, a little like the steering wheel of a car.

Throughout the course of our lives, we sometimes receive Eagle feathers as gifts to honor us. My first Eagle feather came from the tail, and the pipe holder who presented it to me said I would receive it first, because at that time in my life, direction was the thing I needed most. Power would come later when I was mature enough to accept it. Given too soon, and the feather can turn bad. A few years and some sweat lodges later, I received the power wing feather.

South is the yellow summer

We turn clockwise in a circle when we pray, so the next direction is south. It is the season of summer, and its animal is Coyote, according to the ones who taught me.

The color of south is yellow, like the summer sun that warms the breast of Mother Earth. It brings forth the nourishment of tall green corn to feed the people. We hold our sacred objects up to the sky of south and give thanks for surviving the cold winter snows and icy winds to once again see another warm summer of dancing and prosperity. We know that we will prosper, because Father Sky has made the miracles of the recent springtime come to bloom as tiny shoots that grow quickly in the flush of the season.

Knee deep in the strong growth of summer, it warms our face, and children dance and play outside in the balmy pastures of July.

Coyote comes from the golden yellow summer

Coyote, the sacred Trickster, comes to play with everyone who has honored Creation. He tricks the kids into giving away their lunch to the little skinny dog who lies when he tells them he is starving. He is not so skinny. He has just come from a swim in the river, so his thick fur is wet and sticks to him, making him look quite pathetic. Coyote is a liar, cheat, and thief. But he is also the keeper of funny stories and clowning around, which has its rightful place in the balance of our lives.

We need to caution ourselves about humor, so that we maintain the ability to discern truth from lies, and to protect ourselves from any magic that calls the dark forces. Coyote warns us to hold our dignity and respect close to our sacred heart, lest we lose ourselves in a joke, and our soul to a lie. The Trickster also illustrates stealing, and too much desire for things that do not belong to us. For instance, if we were to steal the wing feathers from the sacred lodge, the power of those wings would hurt us. When we are ready for those things, they will come to us. When Coyote makes mischief, he always bites himself in the ass. Coyote comes with the golden yellow summer sun from the south.

The west of darkness

Turning clockwise, we enter the west, the direction of darkness, the great void, death, and dreams. When we offer sacred objects to the sky of the west, we see the color black before us. The sun sets in the west, bringing darkness and nurturing sleep for healing the mind, body, and spirit.

West, being directly across from east in the circle of Creation, seems mysterious because it is difficult to see in the dark. Yet we honor the black of night because it holds the greatest of our dreams, and the formation of our spirituality. If fear lives among us in the west, we ask Coyote of summer to steal it for us, and bring it into the light so it can be examined.

The season is autumn, say my teachers, and we do not go there without Creation's helpers to assist. Our journey into the unknown will come when we are mature enough to handle it. It is an observance we honor as we move through the rights of passage, the seasons of our own lives.

Bear from the west sleeps and dreams

Bear lives in the west. He sleeps throughout the dark time. He goes to his cave of dreams in late fall. In the early autumn, though, he gathers food and eats great quantities so he can fatten up for the winter. Bear's natural diet is vegetarian. He is not really a predator, but has been given great gifts of protection by Grandfather so that he is able to enter his cave without fear of the dark, and so that he may walk the earth without fear of predators.

When we learn to meditate and experience a brief moment of loneliness before bonding with the Creator, that moment is the doorway to the great void. It is what stands between us and Creation. Bear dreams the greatest dreams because he sleeps longer than anyone. So we not only honor west, but also the dreams of Bear because in the darkness is the knowledge of everything sacred. We only visit the sacred mysteries as our deeper selves when we dream. We do not die, though, until we understand everything Grandfather wants us to experience as humans.

As loved ones pass through the void into the Faraway, we cannot see their life anymore, and we grieve for the loss we feel. Because it is dark in the void of west, we think those who have passed over are missing. But they are in the Faraway and we will see them at a great ceremony when we, too, pass over.

Dreams help us shape our reality if we honor them without fear. We do well to journal our dreams and share them with a holy man who has the gift of understanding them. Every dreamer and visionary among our people follows closely the interpretation of the elder with whom he or she shares the dreams. It is not possible for us alone to discern the dreams of this sacred experience.

North is winter purification

As we turn from west in a clockwise direction, we face north, the place of winter purification. The color (or noncolor) is white, like the snow that covers the mountain. A secondary color of the winter is sometimes blue. Blue is the color that shadows the high drifts of snow that freeze time, and provide a doorway to the dream place. Blue is the coolest color, and as we watch the shadows we remember the Creation, migration, and rights-of-passage stories told by the older relatives of the tribes. It is the time of year when we huddle near the fire in the lodge with our families and retell these stories.

We take stock of our lives. Have we done well in the other seasons? Will our stores of food last through the sacred purification? Have we enough wood to keep us from the death that so often comes with winter?

The center of winter brings a ceremony when we stand barefoot on the snow and pray for the strength to continue the journey to spring. We stay close to our elders and keep them warm as we stand in the snow, because we are never quite sure if we can pass on the stories of our people as well as they can. But at the same time, if they die, we know the Grandfathers will give us their gift if we have honored them in a good and sacred way.

Winter marks the seriousness of passing time, and reminds us that we are to use every day to the best of our talents and gifts.

Mountain Lion is of the north

The animal of the north is the Mountain Lion, the keeper of independence and purity through inner and outer strength. The one who walks the boundaries of the earth now is Mountain Lion with her heavy winter coat. She sharpens her claws on the bark of ponderosa pine and drinks from the small portions of the river that do not freeze. She never takes more than she needs from the land, lest she use up the last of her provisions. She is a predator who silently stalks the four-legged creatures who play and scamper around among the swirling snow. Her yellow-gold eyes provide the only light that is hope throughout the winter purification.

She raises her young playfully with great purpose, and teaches them to fight so that they will fulfill their native call as warriors of the natural world. She honors the silence because Grandfather has given her spiritual sight to look deep into dreams. She is a spirit chaser, according to my elders. She runs faster than anyone on the mountain, and she loves passionately. It is her strength, passion, and spiritual gifts that enable her to reign over the harsh winter environment.

Mountain Lion is the loner who walks in silent ceremony. She knows herself, and possesses sacred knowledge that comes to her from the songs of the frozen wind.

While she roams, and life from the previous years ends, those who weather the frozen storms of north enter the dream time with Bear. We are quiet when we think of the sleeper in his cave, so that we may honor him as he dreams the great knowledge for us who understand that divine wisdom comes from those dreams.

The supernatural directions

The three remaining directions we honor—up, down, and the present moment—call the powers of the supernatural to join us with the winds of Mother Earth. To them, we also offer sacred objects to the sky.

The direction of up

We continue to offer the sacred object used for the four directions as we honor the direction of the sky, which remains a mystery, because it goes on forever. It must be a type of circle with no beginning and no end.

It was always there, and always will be, say the old ones. This is the direction where we recognize the Creator, because only He could possibly comprehend the vastness of eternity. We see from the natural world around us that Father Sky and Mother Earth are separate, yet one, through spiritual bonding. One is male and the other female. The female is the mother of our physical lives and the keeper of the healing herbs. The other is the Creator, the Great Father.

People have tried to describe the Creator, or Father Sky, some in vivid detail. Indians, though, don't see Him in a physical sense. What we "see" is how gently he guides and loves us as we honor him throughout our lives. The Great Spirit continually reveals Himself to us through healing, knowledge, visions, dreams, rights of passage, and gifts from our Mother Earth.

As we offer gratitude to the Creator and honor his partner, the womb of Mother Earth, we are richly blessed by both. According to my dad, if you wanted to know Father Sky, walk with respect for your Mother Earth, and she will introduce you to her mate.

One of the miracles of the sky, which we honor as one of the seven directions, are the stars. Grandfather put them there to lead people in the right directions. If we cannot find our way in the daytime, how can we possibly find our way in the dark? In the dark, the gift of true direction comes beautifully alive with the constellations. Humans have used them for thousands of years throughout the world to navigate themselves to a desired destination. We still do.

Down, the Mother Earth

Our earthly nourishment comes from the sacred earth. The soil is the womb of life. Grandma Shaken' Skunk told me that every herb we will ever need to heal from the diseases of humankind grows within a two-mile radius of any mountain slope.

From the Creator's teachings we learn to brew the teas of healing in our dreams and visions. These are gifts from the sacred union of Mother Earth and Father Sky. Anyone can mix herbal remedies, but the healing channel of Creation comes through knowledge of ceremony.

We are not all called as healers or storytellers. But those who are have a grave responsibility to respect this call in a good way, which is constantly being scrutinized by native elders. If we fail to honor Creation, the gifts will be taken away and given to someone more deserving. If we sell them for a price, they become corrupt, and must be righted through the giveaway (see Chapter 11).

So we offer sacred objects to Mother Earth in a downward direction, the sixth direction. This provides the union between the material and the spiritual that brings the ceremony together. As we face each direction, we ask Grandfather to send us the wisdom from each of these places. We draw power from these directions, say my teachers. The power, though, does not belong to us, but to the ceremony. Most Indians don't claim to own power. We only use it when needed, according to Creation's laws of nature, which we do not claim to fully understand.

Gravity and Mother Earth

Another gift of Mother Earth is gravity. By the laws of physics, the gifts of gravity can be mostly understood, except for the question of why. Why were we brought together here on this planet to love one another and dance the sacred dance? The only answer my native teachers could think of is because something much greater than us must love us very much.

We are a community of humans, diverse in every possible way. Yet, gravity helps to hold us all together on the great lodge of Mother Earth. The surface of the earth has every product we need to eat, build our homes, heal ourselves, create great works of art, stay warm, and enjoy ourselves. This is enough to keep us busy and happy for a lifetime if we are willing to honor and respect all living things and each other.

The environment and Mother Earth

Native Americans are the first environmentalists. It is the old ways of our people to follow the laws set down by a loving mother figure. We acknowledge appreciation to the mother of us for the great strong mountains beneath our feet that represent the power and development of life.

☞ We thank the union of earth and sky that moves the deep oceans and powerful rivers that carve the slope of the continents of our birth.

☞ We thank Creation in the place of the earth for the clouds that recycle precious water into the solvent of the human body, mind, and spirit.

☞ We thank the power of fire that cleans the land of debris in its natural recycling of the extreme forces of her elements, and that provides light and heart necessary for survival.

☞ We thank the winds that move the seed of new life from place to place to replenish new growth of food, wood, and herbal medicines.

☞ We thank the winds and rivers for the singing among secret places of nature that spell the ancient songs of our people.

☞ We offer up every part of nature expressing gratitude for it in creative ways. Before we have the right to ask for anything, we need to show humble gratitude for all we have been given.

☞ We do not forget the healing herbs Mother Earth has given us as we offer our sacred objects downward to her in ceremony.

☞ We ask for the wisdom expressed by the earth as she moves through the cycles of the season, recycling everything she is capable of renewing.

☞ We ask that the trash we accumulate in the form of resentments, fear, and other defects of character be recycled into the topsoil of fresh new life.

☞ We desire from the earth that the energy we have invested into the poisons, pollution, and toxic wastes of our hearts be used to grow a tree or fill a river with the songs of the old ones.

These things we ask for when we offer the sacred objects in the down direction during the part of the ceremony that calls for the sacred wisdom from the seven directions.

Living the moment: The seventh direction

Last of all, we offer the sacred objects to the center of the seven directions—the here and now, the present moment.

We are the sum total of everything we have ever experienced in this physical life up until now. Every desire, fear, hope, sorrow, all the laughter, pain, searching, finding, and trying of every new thing and every new relationship becomes past of the present movement. The greatest teachers we have ever had are love and pain. Love has filled and renewed us every time we hold it in our heart. It has made us want more love. It has been said that love's only desire is to fulfill itself.

Pain, though, is the touchstone of spiritual growth. Pain is that stirring force that desires change and requires strength to be overcome in any manifestation of itself in mind, body, or spirit. Pain is not only physical. Sometimes we walk through spirit-filled pain—we walk through the fire—to find ourselves.

The here and now is everything that we are holistically. We express gratitude at this point in the ceremony for everything we have received, everything that has been taken from us, and everything we have left.

Understanding in preparation for the 7 directions

If we find ourselves honoring the seven directions in the ways just discussed, it is because we have reached a level of understanding that calls us to do so. By the time we reach the seventh direction, we are focused and grateful enough to participate in ceremony.

☞ East is the direction for beginning our prayer for any type of ceremony. The sunrise represents new beginnings and springtime. The color of east is red, representing the blood of life and passion. The east's animal is Eagle, who flies higher than any bird in the United States, so she can look down with objectivity.

☞ South comes next as we move clockwise. The color for south is yellow, which represents the heat-giving season of summer. It brings the corn to life to feed the people. Summer is a time for dances of gratitude by those who have survived the icy cold winds of winter. Coyote, the trickster, plays outside in the summer to teach us how to trick ourselves if we fool around too much. But he also reminds us to have a sense of humor.

☞ West is the next continuum of the circle. West is black and takes us to void of sacred mysteries, the unknown. As the direction of night, it represents dreams, visions, and death. Bear is west's animal, the keeper of sacred dreams. We honor the slumber of Bear, who prepares for hibernation in the west, the season of autumn.

☞ White, like snow, is the color of north, next in the circle of no end. Time for the sacred purification of Mother Earth in this season of Winter. The animal of northern winter is Mountain Lion, the keeper of her territory and of the medicine, which will remain alive for the people as they tell stories inside the lodge around a warm fire.

☞ Up toward the sky is honored as the direction of the Creator's lodge. He is sometimes called "Father Sky" in ceremony. He is the mate who brings Mother Earth to be the other half of His ability to create life.

☞ Down toward the earth in honoring the directions means to honor the marriage of Creation. By this loving union we observe the greatest understanding of all: we are not merely physical beings seeking a spiritual experience, but actually spiritual beings seeking a physical experience, as does Father Sky in His bonding with Mother Earth.

☞ The center of Creation being honored as the seventh direction is the here and now. This very moment is the most important time of our lives, especially if we are in ceremony. It is the time we honor the creation of ourselves and those in our prayer circle. By offering the sacred objects of material and spiritual value to the circle, we can achieve great wisdom and healing.

7

PLANNING A
TALKING CIRCLE CEREMONY

The talking circle as we know it today is a modern version of what was once called the council fire. Council fires were usually called by a member of the tribe who was wrestling with a problem and needed the advice of the elders and medicine people.

Today's talking circle is used in a number of different ways. For instance, a memorial hospital in Arizona conducts a weekly talking circle for Native Americans with diabetes from a nearby Indian reservation in an effort to combine traditional practices with Western medical treatment; Alaskan students at a multicultural education conference used the talking circle to share ideas about how to preserve language and culture; and talking circles are used by various faiths for interfaith dialogues.

Talking circles have also taken to the airwaves and the Web. The American Indian Court Judges Association conducts a tribal court talking circle to encourage online participation in the tribal justice system; and American Indian Radio On Satellite (AIROS), with 53 affiliate radio stations, boasts the first on-air talking circle.

Even with the modernization of the talking circle, though, many of the old ways are still incorporated into them, particularly those for private ceremonies.

Yesterday's council fire

Everyone who attended brought a piece of wood, rather than someone supplying an entire cord. That way, everyone received equal warmth from the sacred fire.

Those attending passed around a sacred object, or icon, such as an Eagle feather. It was passed clockwise so that all shared the problem they were there to discuss. Everyone was considered an expert on the problem and its solution, so all participants were honored equally. As the feather passed, the individual holding it was the only one who had the right to speak and be listened to. No one was to interrupt as the person spoke. As participants spoke, solutions to the problem were dispensed.

Other spiritual icons with positive energy could be used because some tribes honor birds other than Eagle, and may want to use feathers from those birds. Another popular item used was the 'talking stick.' It could be a plain stick, or one decorated with objects symbolizing something of significance to those attending the circle. The objects passed around could also symbolize personal prayers.

I've taken part in talking circles where rocks that had special meaning to the person requesting the ceremony have been used in place of the talking stick or feather. The explanation for the use of the rock as a symbol can be very poignant. Rocks are believed to be the oldest living beings by many native people.

Other objects with special meaning can also serve as a "talking stick."

Today's talking circle

Yesterday's council fire has evolved to today's talking circle. A large fire in the center is no longer needed, although, it can still be used. Chairs can be arranged in a circle to accommodate the number of people attending. At my home, we usually use a talking stick, because the gatherings are intertribal, with most attending not Indian. We may include five or six native people, and 15 to 20 from other cultures and religions.

Prior to the circle, everyone invited has been told of the particular talking circle's purpose. Also, all those invited for the first time will find at least one person they know, or who has something in common with them. This adds to their comfort. Many who come have never taken part in a native circle previously, and are completely unfamiliar with it. They may be skeptical or nervous about attending. Some fear it will somehow conflict with their own religion, if they have one. Most, however, soon become very comfortable.

To me, the more diversified the makeup of the circle, the more interesting and spiritual the interaction. The only time we pass an Eagle feather is when the attendees are from our own extended family, from tribal members who are extremely old, and very close friends in whose ceremonies we have previously shared.

Other talking circles take place in our home for folks in recovery from alcoholism and drug addiction, and for celebrations throughout the year with others who aren't in recovery, including spiritual leaders, elders, and professional people from every walk of life. These talking circles celebrate such things as birthdays, retirements, anniversaries, and seasonal celebrations such as equinoxes and solstices. We have taken talking circles into schools, churches, and rehabilitation centers. We've conducted them for the purpose of world peace, and for individuals dealing with life changes, crisis, and different phases of their lives, such as puberty, menopause, and growing old.

The wisdom from all participants at these gatherings never fails to help those in need, or to give insight or healing for everyone in the circle.

The talking stick

Part of the talking circle's success is the power of the talking stick, or other icon or symbol. On their first encounter, some people are awed by the idea of being able to have their say without being interrupted.

The stick we use in most of our talking circles is made of willow, and involves special meaning to us. It comes from that used for the construction of a tribal sweat lodge ceremony we once attended. Following the four days of ceremony, my husband asked the holy man if he could have some of the willow when the lodge was taken down. He was given several fine pieces that have been made into talking sticks. The one we use most often has been used for years in all of our circles. It contains Coyote fur on the end of it to symbolize the Trickster in all of us. It calls us to be honest as we share in the circle. We have found that the stick makes it nearly impossible for anyone in the circle to lie.

Long black hair from the tail of a horse also hangs from the stick to symbolize the animal used for centuries to carry people to their desired destination. Through this symbol, our prayer is that we will be carried to the destination of wisdom and sacred knowledge according to the will of Creation. The stick is partly wrapped in green hemp rope to symbolize our prayer that we appreciate the evergreens, such as the pinion (of the penon family), pine, and juniper (of the cypress family) that keep the green of their life throughout the harshest winds in the dead of winter. By identifying with these sturdy trees, we ask for courage and strength to endure the trials of life without losing our dignity or integrity.

A strip of wolf hair can be found half way down the stick to remind us to pray for the wisdom of the wolf, the teacher of the animal kingdom. When anyone in the circle holds the stick and speaks, he or she becomes the teacher of that moment for the rest of us.

It never fails that those attending the circle bring the best of themselves to the time they share with the rest of us while holding the stick.

The last object on the stick is a strip of buffalo hair. Buffalo is the answer to the prayer of the ancients asking the Creator to provide them with their physical needs— food, clothing, and shelter. Every part of the buffalo hunted by natives was used. The hide provided the walls for their homes and some of their clothing. The bones were used as tools and jewelry, the sinew for strong chord. The wonderful tasting meat held them through the winter.

When my husband holds the stick and describes the symbols of prayer to our guests, he speaks slowly in a low tone about these things. He says that the stick has turned to a prayer stick over the years because we have seen it answer so many prayers for those who have touched it. He asks that everyone in the circle show respect for these prayers by not allowing any part of the stick to touch the ground.

Sage, the holy herb

We burn sage at the very beginning of the talking circle. We believe the Creator finds the odor of sage pleasing. Also, sage has many medicinal purposes.

In tea it becomes an antispasmodic, astringent used for gastritis, enteritis, and other stomach disorders, and for eliminating mucous congestion. It can also be gargled for sore throat. Sage oil is also believed to inhibit the enzyme acetyl cholinesterase, which may contribute to memory loss and Alzheimer's.

However, one of its greatest uses among Indians is to burn it prior to beginning any ceremony so that we can "bathe" in its smoke to purify ourselves and prevent evil spirits from entering. The sage is often made up of small wrapped bundles. Or its individual leaves can be burned in any type of small fireproof vestibule.

Cedar, sweet grass, and tobacco (sometimes in combination with sage) are also used for purification by some tribes. These also create an odor pleasing to the Creator.

Gathering sage

The fresh sage is gathered in the late spring when the leaves are large, tender, and new. In the Southwest, Mule Ear Sage grows at about 3,400 foot elevations, and Mountain Sage grows at about 6,700 feet. Both are found on mountain slopes, and both are used in native ceremony.

Different types of sage grow throughout the world, and other parts of the United States. Some are a spice for cooking, and other are ornamental flowers, but all belong to the Labiatae (Lamiaceae) or mint family. Gathering is accomplished by various family members, and can be a ceremony of itself. Tobacco is offered to Mother Earth in exchange for the sage. It is sprinkled in a clockwise fashion around the plant. Only about a third of the stems and leaves from the plant are gathered so that we don't injure it, allowing it to come back thicker the next year.

The plants we harvest are in wilderness areas, and in those places undisturbed by the general public. The plants have grown tremendously since we began harvesting them about 20 years ago. I'm sure this has occurred in other areas where Native Americans harvest the sage.

Once the sage is gathered, we offer thanks to Creation, and pray that it will always be used in a good way to heal and cleanse those who burn it. We gather a couple of large trash bags full each year, because we use a great deal of it throughout the seasons.

Bundling the sage

The same day it is gathered and blessed, it is bundled, a process taking several hours because it is accomplished in the old way. We bind a few stems together to form a bundle about 10 inches long, and approximately 2 inches thick. It is tightly wrapped with red thread or yarn to signify the blood of the people.

Wrapping is done in the form of the spiral dance, from the bottom clockwise to the top and back to the bottom, maintaining the clockwise wrap. In this way we send our prayer to the Father Sky, and He sends the results back to Mother Earth. Once the sage is all bundled, we place the neat little packages in a tall basket where they will dry for several weeks. Once dry, they are used in ceremonies of all sort, and as gifts to elders and holy people.

Using sage in the talking circle

The talking circle begins when the sage is lit, and someone of native heritage offers the sage and Eagle feather to the seven directions (see Chapter 6). This part of the ceremony takes as long as the native wants to spend honoring and describing the directions. Then he or she goes around the circle clockwise and smudges each person down for the purpose of purification. Smudging is done with the smoke from the sage bundle and an Eagle feather. The native uses the feather to push the smoke out towards one person at a time from the top of his or her head to the feet, front and back, going clockwise around the circle. If the native doing the smudging becomes aware of any sickness or discomfort in the individual being blessed, he or she may touch them lightly on the head or the heart, or both with the end of the Eagle feather, and pray silently for a healing. Other than this prayer, the native doing the smudging does not touch any member of the circle without their permission, as this can be invasive and unfamiliar to some guests.

Once everyone has been cleansed, the smoldering bundle is placed in a large shell or earthen bowl in the center of the circle so that the prayer continues as long as the sage continues to smoke. Most of the time, smudging is done outdoors when we have guests, because many non-Indian people we invite to our circles are unaccustomed to being in a closed area with smoke.

The prayer

Following the cleansing, a prayer is said. Everyone in the circle comes together with their arms around each other standing in a single circle facing the center. Then the elder begins a prayer of gratitude for the gathering, and all the blessings we get from the circle. If there is a guest of honor, such as a birthday person, or a visiting elder, gratitude is expressed for his or her presence.

The individual chosen to begin a mixed (men and women) talking circle with a spoken prayer is always the oldest traditional male American Indian who is in attendance. This piece of protocol ensures that no one's feelings will be hurt. The only exception is if natives from any of the local tribes of California are present because the ceremony is taking place on their land. This supercedes being the eldest from a tribe in another part of the country.

This example of California is given because that's where I live, but my people are not originally from California. This respect is shown in other parts of the country when a native from somewhere else takes part in ceremony. It not only gives honor and respect to the Indians from the area where the ceremony is taking place, but it honors their ancestors.

The prayer always asks for those gathered to be blessed with wisdom and honesty to share with one another. It is made clear that while we are in the circle, we are one people with no boundaries of color, age, or financial status. Through prayer, we have been united as one tribe. It is suggested that if we have tears for any reason, that we leave them in the circle in exchange for the wisdom we receive.

After the prayer, the host describes the object to be passed around the circle, and everything it stands for.

The feast and the Grandfather plate

A feast is in order following a talking circle. Usually a potluck follows the talking circles that take place at our home. People bring wonderful foods, sometimes from a variety of ethnic cultures. This, of course, is an honor to the Creator.

A prayer of thanks is always given to the Creator, and as the line forms around the banquet table, a plate is first fixed for Grandfather and placed outside.

A friend once asked me what happened to the food placed outside for the Creator. I told her that if the animals carry medicine of the Creator, then they are messengers for the Creator and it gets to Him one way or the other.

Nunda Awi

Nunda Awi has had talking circles to celebrate her birthday since she was 8 years old. She was raised in a traditional family. Some people believe that when children reach about 7 or 8, they develop the ability to decide for themselves the path they will follow. That is the age when freedom of choice is bestowed on them. For that reason, when Nunda Awi reached her 8th birthday, she began to seek the wisdom of the older native women by inviting them each year. For the first two or three years, only family and tribal members attended. After that, she began to see some of her teachers from public school as very wise women, so she began inviting them.

After Nunda Awi received her first moon in her early teens, she began to include men in the circle, because she saw that she could learn most about any future mate she would marry from the older men she admired.

For the next five years, women walked her through the first few years of feminine development. The circles continued until she was grown and had left home.

It was a fine example of how our mentors evolve as we mature. It is also an example of different types of talking circles. They can be mixed, or with women or men only. It depends on the purpose of the circle.

Purpose of the talking circle

The circle has many manifestations, chief among them is unity of mind, body, and soul. The thoughts expressed in a talking circle are not only the ideas coming from the participants, but are made true and strong from the prayers sent to the Creator, and the other six directions. It is all encompassing. Our circle is larger than we can see with our eyes.

☞ The council fire of our elders took place to discuss the problems of their people, and to find solutions. Everyone brought a piece of wood, so that everyone was equalized. All contributed equally and received equal spiritual and physical warmth from the fire. Today, the council fire has evolved into the talking circle where the same spiritual dynamics occur.

☞ The talking stick is used in the circle. It is decorated with symbols that collectively spell a prayer for everyone who attends the talking circle. The stick is passed clockwise around the circle, and each person who shares has the right to speak and the right to be listened to. We never interrupt. Respect and equality is given to everyone in the circle.

☞ Sage is used to purify the participants and the circle. Natives believe the Creator finds the aroma of smoldering sage pleasing, so it is used in the prayers of many of our ceremonies. Just the gathering of sage is a ceremony of itself. An entire day is devoted to the prayers, offerings, gathering, and bundling of sage.

☞ The opening prayer for the talking circle is usually done by the oldest American Indian male in attendance. The only exception is if a native from one of the California tribes from the local area is present. Then it is he who offers the prayer.

☞ A potluck often follows a talking circle. Respect is shown to the Grandfather.

8

Capturing the Vision

Some call it "crying for vision." We seek these visions at different times and at different ages in our lives, but the most well-known seems to be when tribes send their youth out to seek vision as they reach adolescence.

A variety of traditional ways exist to accomplish a vision quest, with some of the old ways taking six months of preparation. There is no one way of achieving the quest. Several ways of using old spiritual practices will be offered. They all achieve the same end.

The main purpose of a quest is to establish a connection with Creation that enables us to know ourselves better and use that knowledge to understand the gifts we have been given by Grandfather.

By aligning our whole selves, good and bad, with the will of Creation we discover simple and comfortable ways to live in harmony with the personal truth of ourselves.

Secrets of the shadows

Earlier, we spoke of the shadowland as though it was an actual place in order to grasp the supernatural arena of faith as something solid, or geographic. Once we have that simple understanding, we are better able to enter the second or advanced stage, which takes us at will into the lodge of sacred knowledge. We learn to use these advanced skills for problem solving, and continued development of spiritual, mental, and physical health, sometimes involving visions.

Visions are gifts that provide answers to questions posed in prayer. The main religions of the world, all of which contain sacred texts or scriptures, were written as groups of stories or directions given to their followers by individuals who had experienced the gift of sacred knowledge within their physical lives.

Many practiced something akin to a vision quest in order to acquire the knowledge of which they wrote. Nearly all of the stories illustrate how the destructive nature of humankind can be turned around. The revelations received by the prophet or visionary showed men and women how to turn poison into medicine.

The sacred stories written in the world's main religions are much like Native American stories. They show us how to live with the issues—good and evil, weakness and strength, hardness and softness—of who we are. They show us how to transcend the problems of the world in hopes of discovering our highest selves in conscious contact with Creation. These religions may define Creation differently from one another, but the likeness of what they had to say are still similar. And the founders of the ways of enlightenment or salvation were all very impressive individuals. As different as they may seem, they all pretty much had the same goals in mind.

The writing of these goals may seem different, even foreign among different belief systems, but they are quite similar. In other words, it may seem we each hold separate or peculiar ways of understanding Creation, but the major differences may only be that our thought processes are different, with the end result being the same.

Yet, as with the native spiritual stories, these visionaries from all parts of the world believe that our physical life is only a temporary state in the circle of eternity. If our place in the scheme of things on earth is only temporary, it makes many of us search for our purpose. That search often leads to the vision quest.

The sacred mountains

My grandmother used to tell us that our family would spend many lifetimes learning the ways of the "sacred mountain." For us, everything holy is within the mountain environment, because this is where our people have lived since the time of Creation.

It is natural to us that we became experts on herbal remedies of the mountain areas, and survival in the pine-covered wilderness, and how to find life in the dead of a frozen winter. But we would be hard-pressed to survive a summer of scalding heat in the Mojave Desert, or the shifting sand dunes of Saudi Arabia.

Now that the world has become smaller through air travel, education, television, and the Internet, we can explore the spirituality of peoples from other lands with ease and with greater understanding. We can come to understand that "sacred mountains" is a metaphor for the sacred, or the shadowlands, whether it be indoors, outdoors, in caves, or even under water.

Vision quest: Doorway to the supernatural

Everything that stands between light and a hard surface casts a shadow.

Pretend that we are experiencing our first day on earth. None have gone before us. We are among the first people. As the sun goes down and it begins to get cold and dark for the first time, we discover the gift of fire, and take it into a cave to keep us warm.

Within the cave, the fire casts strange shadows on the walls as the people move about. The images are distorted. They seem like scary, ghost-like figures of ourselves, but they are not. We learn that they come and go with the fire, and they are gone when we go outside in the morning. This can mean only one thing: the cave is haunted! We won't be sleeping in there again.

Today we know a bit more about the nature of shadows, but perhaps those first experiences of humankind made us suspect that spirits lived among us. Those same types of spirits still charge our bodies.

There is a moment in time when our awareness becomes acute and every nerve is on edge. We are prepared for fight or flight, and we are in a state of what the military calls "combat readiness." Such states can be brought about through practicing martial arts. This kind of awareness is when adrenaline runs fast through us, and we must make a split-second decision regarding our next action. This is the moment that hangs in the balance of dark and light, reality and fiction. Aggression and submission, faith and fear rest on the towering cliff of the shadowland.

This is the moment where logic stops and instinct takes over. It is a suspended moment where the only knowledge available to us is beyond our conscious thought. It is the time we bond with the highest potential of enlightenment and truth. When we've absolutely surrendered and nothing holds us back, we enter the field of divine knowledge.

It is the same experience that we achieve in the vision quest. Native people have cried for vision as long as anyone can remember.

Vision quest questions

These vision quest questions were written by tribal elders. They were given to a friend of mine when he asked the elder to take him to the mountains for a vision quest. We have copied them and used them hundreds of times over the years to help those individuals who come to us seeking connection to their spiritual selves and divine understanding.

They are meant to be thought provoking, and by answering them, we affirm our strengths and weaknesses, thus enabling us to know what types of help to ask for, as we continue our quest for the sacred.

The questions need to be answered by us privately, and in writing. That allows us to be as absolutely honest with ourselves as possible. Before writing any answer, think about it for as long as it takes to give a true answer. Try to use honesty and clarity wrought of feeling and heart, rather than intellectualizing it, as if writing a sermon to be published.

Come from a low place in the self, the "gut," or the place of the child within. Answer in simple terms, so that the answers are clear and precise. Avoid an ethereal philosophy. *Keep it simple.* This is the first step to prepare ourselves for spiritual understanding.

☞ Who or what is my Creator?

☞ What is my relationship with the Creator?

☞ Why was I born?

☞ With what skill or gifts am I blessed?

☞ Am I using my skills and gifts?

☞ Who are my people?

☞ Who are my teachers?

☞ What are the great monsters in my life?

☞ What must I do to face them?

☞ Why must I die?

As we work though these questions, we may want to discuss the answers with someone we look up to spiritually in order to remain objective and honest with ourselves.

Every step we take on this journey is for our own betterment, to make us more whole. We do not go alone into the supernatural. We are not out to punish ourselves.

When natives go on a vision quest, or a similar ritual or planned experience, we ask the spiritual leaders to join us. The elders or others may set up a base camp not far from the place we camp during out time outdoors. They can sneak up and check on us from time to time, or we make a rock pile where they leave water for us each day. We move the rock so they know we retrieved the water and that we are okay. We see no one during this time outdoors. This minimal contact is our way of alleviating our own worries, and those of the people who are nearby.

Finding the right place

Finding the right place for our vision quest is important. We need to be familiar with the area, so that we feel relatively comfortable during our stay. Yet, we also need to get as far into the wilderness as is reasonably possible.

If we are extremely physically fit, we may want to backpack into a wilderness area. If we are less familiar with being in the outdoors, it's okay to just walk a mile or so from the base camp. Whatever our destination, it should be about the same altitude to which we are accustomed. It's not a good idea to travel from a home elevation of 4,000 feet, and enter a mountainous area of 7,000 feet or more. The change in elevation can exhaust a person before he or she even begins the quest.

If you live in a mountain area already, that terrain is perfect. If you're used to a desert or plains area, or the beach, try to find a spot similar to what you are used to, but isolated. The reason for selecting a place similar to what we are accustomed to is that our bodies have become acclimatized not only to its altitude, but to its weather, flora, and fauna.

The experience will include fasting, staying alone without the benefit of shelters, and entering into unfamiliar states of mind. It's purpose is to "succeed," so we don't set ourselves up for any more difficulty than is absolutely necessary. It's not a survival of the fittest challenge.

If possible, it's a good idea to use the acreage of someone you know, if it's large enough to provide a "getting away" place. Even a closed campground, if available, is good. Natives often use the backwoods of their reservation land, which is not available to the general public. Sometimes if a request is made through someone who is known by tribal leaders to use a certain spot of their land for a friend's vision quest, it will be granted. But it really raises the ire of Indians when someone trespasses on their land.

Also, some national forest lands run into private property, so it is necessary to make careful plans, including the proper permissions for a place, before starting on a quest.

Once the area has been selected, camp there first with friends, and familiarize yourself with the land. Walk around and check the place out thoroughly a few times until it feels comfortable to be there. This will be your home alone for two to four days. Once familiar and not fearful of the land, your time during the quest can be spent capturing the best of your spiritual life, a connection with the most high Creator.

Provisions for the vision quest

In times past, folks trekked to the mountain with nothing more than a buffalo hide and a knife. We realize that today most of us are not quite that rugged. We still try to keep our needs as simple as possible, but our health needs to be considered as we prepare to fast, pray, and commune with the elements in a natural setting.

If we are reasonably healthy, a two-day stay will require a pair of sturdy boots, layered clothing with heavy jacket and gloves, a sleeping bag, and a large supply of water.

For those with medical conditions, especially if it requires daily medication, it's advisable to consult a physician before embarking on such a journey. Once our health has been taken care of, it adds to our feeling of safety, and we can proceed with no self doubts. Again, a well-planned trip, taking everything into consideration in advance, means that we can devote our time to receiving the fullness of the quest. If we are worrying about other things, it dilutes the experience.

We don't take books, or any other form of amusement, but it's okay to pack a journal and pen. We have chosen a time of year when it's not below freezing at night, so there is no need for a tent. When we are not asleep, we need to be able to look at the stars and at the silhouettes of the natural environment.

The time

I like to go out during a full moon for four reasons:

☞ Night visibility is better.

☞ More animals are skittering about.

☞ Our spiritual awareness is more acute during a full moon.

☞ Emotions run hotter and faster, and our metabolism is usually slightly elevated.

Focus

Once in our chosen environment, we are going to focus entirely on the natural world. We don't want to become distracted by anything at all that will subtract from our greatest teacher, the wilderness.

Take absolutely no mind altering chemicals or alcohol. These substances only serve to distort our perceptions and deaden senses, which need to be at their peaks for us to accomplish our task. If we are required by a medical condition to take such drugs as prescription pain killers or antidepressants, we might want to postpone the trip until we can accomplish it, even a short stay, without any drugs, even prescription ones. We need all of our fully functioning instincts.

We experience moments of sadness, laughter, fear, and divine love. These feelings can range from mild to extreme. Such reactions must be completely unencumbered if the quest is to be of value to us. If we are unable to go and stay alone in the vastness of the outdoors for a couple of days, Chapter 10 will guide you on the use of connecting with nature and the spiritual, during a day trip or a hike in a natural environment.

Fasting

Fasting for the purpose of a vision quest can be accomplished in various ways, with the most strict being water only.

For a water only, I recommended steam distilled waters, because if we are going to an extreme fast, it may as well be productive. Steam distilled water is completely without minerals, pollution, or other ingredients. It is the purest form of water, and will cleanse the internal body in the most effective possible way, reaching into the metabolic system.

Provided we are very healthy, and feel sure of ourselves, a four-day fast on the mountains is top of the line. More spiritual work can be accomplished in four days than all other forms of self-improvement or vision seeking.

The first time I went to the mountain for four days, my health would not permit me to fast with water only, so I used fruit juices. It turned out to be more of a cleansing than a fast, but it did the trick. Considering the way I usually love to eat, the fruit juice cleansing was extreme for me at that time of my life.

A good fast can cost us some weight, so this needs to be taken into consideration as a health issue. Many Americans can usually withstand a 5- to 10-pound weight loss with no problems (myself included), so a fast can actually be a good thing for our bodies. But for someone who is underweight, a fast might need some careful thought.

However we fast, we need to be able to feel it. We give up as much intake of nutrition as we can possibly withstand without injuring ourselves. The body uses an incredible amount of energy to digest food. It is not uncommon for a regular meal to take as long as three days to move through the digestive process and be eliminated. Different types of food take measurably different amounts of time for the body to assimilate and completely digest. If the body is working on even a little digestion, it slows down our reaction time. Like a drug, food deadens the mind by turning the attention of the metabolic functions to the lower regions of the body, and away from the brain and the spiritual abilities.

Meat is one of the slowest and most difficult foods to digest. Any other animals products, such as cheese, eggs, and other milk products are next in line for difficulty in digesting. Nuts are also difficult to digest, and can be very high in protein.

The activity of the liver, pancreas, gallbladder, and small intestine is vigorous in the digestion of heavy proteins from any animal products. If we are accustomed to eating meat and other animal products or nuts, we need to practice giving them up prior to a vision quest.

Breads and grains are next in difficulty to digest and the length of time required to assimilate them. As we move on to easier items to digest, vegetables are next. Fresh vegetables are extremely nutritious and much easier to digest than proteins and grains. In the right combinations, they provide enough amino acids for all the proteins we will ever need. The vegetable proteins are easier for the body to use.

Amino acids are the building blocks of protein. During the digestion process, the body is required to break down the crude proteins of meat and animal protein into amino acids, and to reconstruct them into usable, life-sustaining proteins. This demands an extra process in the digestion time of foods. The amino acids of properly combined vegetables, however, need only be assembled once in the digestive process, so this is why some claim they are better for our health.

Fresh fruit is the easiest of all foods to digest. If the human body is completely empty of any type of food in the digestive tract, fruit will only take 15 to 20 minutes to digest. If we live only on fruit for a few days, the mind reaches a level of activity second to none, except when the fast is water only. Also, many food allergies can be eliminated with certain types of fresh fruit cleanses.

Every person's body is different, so we each need to determine for ourselves what is best for us. Try some experimentation. For someone who has never fasted, a cleansing or fast can be an enlightening and life-changing experience for the body, mind, and spirit. Imagine combining a journey of the body, mind, and soul with a vision quest leading to the Spirit of Creation.

Creating the ceremony

Once we have assembled everything we need to take with us, and have done all the necessary research to make the trip, we begin the ceremony of preparing to leave home for a few days.

We gather all our provisions together and offer them to the seven directions in prayers of eager gratitude. We are about to enter into an entire prayer experience, and all the things that help us to make the journey are of great importance—everything from the small backpack to the clothes, pen and paper are blessed before we leave. My husband and I also smudge the car down with sage before we leave on any kind of pilgrimage of this type.

Sometimes my husband drives and drops me off at the desired place, and other times I drive myself and meet other elders there at the base camp before I begin my journey. Once I took the train halfway across the country and walked a very long distance to my camp in preparation for a four-day vision quest.

I have cried for vision in the red desert mesas of New Mexico on the reservation, the vortex-filled mountains of Arizona, pine covered mountains of the Sierra Nevada, the local mountains in Big Bear, California, and even in a few monasteries. The preparations are always the same. Fasting and deep devotions of prayer mark the beginning of the journey.

The first spiritual investment I make is "no expectations." I do not expect to have visions, dreams, or extraordinary revelations of any sort. I expect some loneliness, perhaps sadness or tears, possibly fear, hunger, and impatience. I am usually not disappointed by these selfish expectations that nearly always accompany me on the first day or so.

After leaving the base camp, and saying goodbye to the elders, loved ones, directors, or whomever is waiting at the base camp, we begin our trek to the spot we have selected. Once there, we can arrange rocks in a large circle or ceremonial areas where we will be spending most of our time. All provisions go inside the circle. We can move the circle every day, or we can stay in one spot. The less we have brought with us, the less of the material world we have to think about. I usually start with a prayer to the Creator honoring the seven directions with any spiritual object of worship I have brought with me. Then I look around and take in as much as I can from my spot.

Journaling

Next comes some journaling, which is important because we can't remember everything that passes before us during our quest. As I journal, I ask:

☞ How do I feel now that I am here?

☞ How am I affected by my surroundings?

☞ How am I affected by thoughts that may pass through my mind, no matter how weird they may seem?

Mourning our losses at the spiritual crossroads

During the vision quest, one of the emotions we experience is sadness. This is to be expected because, along with joy and many other emotions, sadness is part of life. Sadness can be a special time, and if faced honestly, it opens the door to increased growth. It forces us to acknowledge the place we are at, which is none other than the spiritual crossroads.

The more honest we are at this point about our fears, self pity, and other regrets, the more we become cleansed.

The first time we venture into nature and experience this vast sadness, it can be nearly devastating. So we need to remember that the emotions related to sadness are only "feelings," not the "us" of ourselves. They are negative parts of our lives, not our lives. They are not the physical reality of what we are experiencing during the quest. And they cannot hurt us. They are actually tools of awakening, because once acknowledged, we can cleanse them.

Another type of sadness can be unresolved grief over the loss of someone dear to us who died, or for some other reason has moved out of our life. We may have experienced the loss a long time ago, but if we never fully mourned it, we can do that in the vastness of nature.

Most of us carry these pockets of grief, often precipitated by misplaced guilt. Sometimes we cry, often quite hard, but on the quest, we are safe so we let the feelings out and leave our tears on the sacred Mother Earth. After all, isn't the idea of a compassionate mother who takes our tears and gives us love in return one of the most comforting metaphors we can imagine?

Many times, sadness and regrets are the very things that hold us back from a connection with the sacred. Our Creator, though, never laughs at us, or demeans our emotions. He is larger and more capable of embracing all of our sorrow than we can ever imagine.

Once we release our feelings, we may feel drained or tired, but we become cleaned through this necessary and life-sustaining process.

We write of these things, our telling of sadness, our experience at shedding grief, in our journal. Later, when we read it back to ourselves, we will plainly see how important it was for us to let go of these sad things.

Listening and watching ceremony

During our stay at the place of our quest, we need to be as vigilant as possible. What is the weather we are experiencing like? Do we need to put on more or fewer clothes? How is our water supply?

Is now a good time for listening, or is it a good time for sleeping? We can sleep, drink water, change clothes, listen for sounds, watch Grandfather Sky at any time we want. There is no schedule on our quest. If we are tired, we sleep. It's as simple as that. If we dream, we try to remember it, and write whatever we can remember of the dream in our journal.

Later, all the things we experience during our quest will come together, even though what is happening at the time seems disjointed, out of focus, unscheduled, and fluid.

We are in a constant state of cleansing. We are often sustaining ourselves with water only. Also, letting go of sadness, thinking about the things that make up our lives (some of which we may decide to let go of), and the vastness of our surroundings in the outdoors lightens our head and cleanses our thoughts.

As we look about, have our surroundings been altered in any way? Is the area immediately around us beginning to feel like a kind of temporary home? We will sleep here tonight. How do we feel about this? Write these impressions in the journal.

The longer we spend outside, the more we hear. Is there a breeze, or the sound of birds or water nearby? Nature is not as quiet as we once may have thought. What once appeared to be a quiet place is really quite filled with sounds, many sounds. As we continue the process of emptying the mind of day-to-day thoughts, our hearing becomes heightened.

☞ Relax in your circle.

☞ Breathe deeply.

☞ As you breathe in, imagine you are breathing with Creation.

☞ As you exhale, let out any toxic feelings like fear or past insults.

☞ Offer this exhale to the earth.

☞ If still or restless, take a moment to walk around or do some exercises to release any uncomfortable feelings.

☞ Take a drink of water if necessary.

☞ Listen as you have never listened before.

☞ What do you hear?

☞ Close your eyes and meditate on the sounds around you.

☞ Can you hear your heartbeat? So you hear animals?

☞ Watch what goes on about you.

☞ Is the light changing now?

☞ Do you see any animals?

☞ Can you see things moving in a breeze—a leaf, a bit of dust?

☞ Record the thoughts of what you hear, see, and feel.

We've been out here for a few hours, so we may feel some hunger in the pit of our stomach. How does our world look as our body changes and the sun or moon moves to another part of the sky?

If the lack of food or addictive substances we may normally use, such as coffee, chocolate, or sugar starts to make us feel weak, or if the lack brings on a headache, what we need is sleep. Our bodies may go through a little detoxification we weren't expecting. But the experience can alert us to addictions to foods or substances that aren't good for us anyway. We needn't worry about the symptoms we may be experiencing, because they make the quest all the more interesting and effective.

Most of our time during the quest is involved in more positive enlightenment than our eating habits. We are listening and watching in order to learn from Creation. Have we seen any animals or insects? All of these life forms, including trees, bushes, rocks or water are our teachers. Earth, air, fire, and water are the teachers of the natural world, and we will remember their voices for a long time after we return home.

Fill your journal with your discoveries of the natural world.

Trusting the Creator

The sensations we are experiencing on our quest are mitigated by the knowledge that we are in the company of our highest Source of Reality—Creation, with whom we can talk at any time of our choosing. Talk also to Mother Earth. Tell her what you think about this phenomenal experience you have undertaken. At the same time, express your gratitude to Creation for all you have, and all you will receive from the experience. Talking with Creation and Mother Earth helps to increase our awareness of everything going on about us. Notice that the living plants shed their leaves and bark. Notice how it disintegrates and disappears into the soil to provide nutrition for new living plants and small insects around it.

We are witness to the truth that nothing ever dies, and through this knowledge, our awareness of the Greatness of Things increases.

After a while of this sort of observation, we develop, experientially, an understanding of the Maker of us all, and we begin to ask questions that we have wondered about for a lifetime.

☞ How can we best serve ourselves and each other in a way that bonds us with the highest Power of all?

☞ Do we need healing from anything?

These are only a couple of the questions we may ask, and for our answers, we look for any in the environment around us. Those answers will unfold before our eyes and ears if we trust in the quest of our vision.

We have lived with the silence of self and Creation for a while now. The answers to personal protection, healing, and spiritual prosperity are all around us. We stay long enough to understand the divine message of the natural world. Some may be more difficult to accept than others. Yet, we accept and surrender to the highest ability of our understanding. Some of the lessons we absorb will seem very simple and obvious after a couple of days outdoors. We will wonder how we ever missed them when we first began our quest.

Accepting the gifts

Once an elder native of the orient decided to go out to the mountain and do exactly what you will be doing for the vision quest—to grow spiritually. He sat in front of a huge old tree whose branches reached down toward the earth. He focused intensely on the area in front of the tree in deep meditation. After a while, a large lion came and sat down beside the tree and looked straight at him. The elder was not afraid because he was a holy man who had bonded with Creation many times. He instinctively knew the lion would not harm him if he did not release the scent of fear from his skin. (Many native people have also developed the ability to offer themselves to nature in this way, and we can too.) The elder did not move and continued to watch.

After a while longer, a large snake came into the elder's field of vision at the base of the tree. The huge snake began to silently move up the trunk, keeping his eyes fixed on the lion, climbing without a sound into the branches. The elder continued to watch and listen without moving, deep in meditation. The snake finally reached a branch directly across from the lion's head. Snake never made a sound as he moved every muscle in his body in perfect harmony with his focus on the lion.

*The lion continued to stare at the elder. Balance,
the elder thought. Snake had perfect balance, focus,
and concentration. Using every muscle in
synchronicity, the snake coiled. With one perfect,
silent move he struck a single fatal blow to the head
of the lion, killing him.*

The elder learned much from his trip to the mountain
that day. The vision quest of that elder happened a couple
of thousand years ago. The elder from his vision of the
movement of snake developed the martial art called Tai
Chi, which involves the spiritual and the physical bonding
together to execute the highest abilities of the human body.

It involves slow, precise movement which focuses all
the attention on awareness and self defense. The spiritual
experience of Tai Chi moves the body as a result of mas-
tering *Chi,* the spirit of Creation within us. We see that
Chi is actually the most creative force of our lives, and
that the body will indeed follow the spirit if it is properly
taught.

So what exactly happened to the elder on the mountain that day. Was the lion real? Or the snake? Or were
these visions from the mind of the elder? If it was a vision,
we might ask, *What is a visionary?*

Is a visionary someone who sees things that are not
there, or someone who perceives the things we see all the
time in a different way than the rest of us?

It is for us alone to decide. But rather than spending
our time deciding which it is, maybe we need to accept the
idea that this person went to the mountain and received
information in some sacred way that still changes the lives
of many people today. Tai Chi gives them confidence in
themselves, and the courage to overcome the physical
shortcomings of their lives. This is as true for us, as it is
the Tai Chi Master.

Our personal vision quests teach us many things that we can use in the here and now. We might learn the art of healing others, self protection, personal and spiritual power, and secrets of financial success. What we learn more importantly, is that it isn't just what sits before us in the future that matters. Nothing we have ever done previously is wasted, good or bad. We are the total sum of everything we have done and learned. Every memory is stored in the recesses of the brain, and every experience is useful in some part of our lives. There is no such thing as a waste of time. Every second has a purpose.

Back to the shadowland

In our own shadowland, our own vision quest, did we believe what we saw? And just what did we see? No two vision quests are ever alike. Each of them shows us our personal exceptional gifts that wait to be discovered on the mountain.

The problem is, many of us are reluctant to accept the gifts we receive from Creation. To help us accept the gifts, we need to fully understand what happened up there. We take our journal writings from our quest to a spiritual advisor for help in discerning them. We pray with this individual, and we ask our Creator to guide the spiritual advisor as he helps us interpret our journey.

After we ask someone to help us, we pray alone. First we give thanks for the opportunity to grow with Creation. Next we ask Grandfather to help us in our newest journey of acceptance, that of our willingness to accept our vision, and use it in the next part of our lives.

Acceptance is always the answer to any "vision" or knowledge we receive, not only on our vision quest, but at other times.

We can go outdoors any time we want to ask for these things and watch for the answers that come from Mother Earth, the true mate of our Creator. It will always be given.

What we have learned of the vision quest

During a vision quest we create an environment of learning and acceptance. We offer the best and the worst of ourselves to the highest possible understanding we can achieve. We are ready for a new type of understanding, and are willing to achieve the goal we set for ourselves.

☞ Secrets of the shadows provide awakenings when we place ourselves in the realm of the supernatural. They assist us in achieving our highest thinking, and another way of perceiving our reality. They help us discover ourselves as we stand between the light and the other side, or the source of the shadow.

☞ The questions for the vision quest make us think about our beliefs, and to affirm it in writing. Before we can understand ourselves we need to define our belief system, rather than change it. If our answers are honest, we can offer it in prayer to the face of Creation when we meet later in nature.

☞ Finding the right place for our vision quest is vital to our peace of mind, and our physical safety. We want to avoid trespassing on private property, and to find a place of similar altitude to where we live. We want to place to be as far into the wilderness as we can get.

☞ Provisions for the vision are the essential things we decide to take with us on the quest.

We take as little as possible to survive, but enough so that our physical health and mental needs are met.

☞ It's important to have experienced fasting or cleansing before we go into nature where we will have nothing to eat for an extended period of time. We need to know about different foods and how long we decide to abstain from them. Our health must always be considered. The quest is not an attempt to punish ourselves, but rather to enlighten us.

☞ The way we arrange our time, provisions, and prayer serves our highest good. We pray over everything we take with us, and offer it to the seven directions because it will sustain us. We create our own circle of rocks and it becomes the lodge in which we will spend most of our time during the days ahead.

☞ Mourning our losses is the surrender to the sadness, fears, and regrets we bring to the ceremony. We let out the loneliness we feel and offer our tears to Mother Earth. She is a kind mother, and will help us feel cleansed when we are honest. No need exists to hold back because our feelings, which are sacred to the Creator. We are in a safe place and there is nothing to fear.

☞ The listening and watching ceremony is the way we focus on the natural world around us, which contains more sounds and sights than we ever imagined. We bring together watching and listening to form a contemplation of the sacred. Creation waits to speak to us of the sacred.

☞ Accepting the gifts of our vision is usually not easy, especially when the gifts are not what we expect. But if we open ourselves to Creation and consult a spiritual advisor to help us interpret the gifts we have received, we will move forward, even though we do not always understand the messages that come from the Faraway. We never need learn these things all by ourselves.

9

FEELING THE EARTH BENEATH OUR FEET

Shaken' Skunk, my grandma, used to say that when we're confused about anything, just go outside and remove our shoes. Walk barefoot on Mother Earth and she will dispel your confusion.

As we make our way across the rocks, thorns, and other plant life, it's natural to seek out the clearest and easiest path we can find to take us out of our confusion.

The problems on your path will insult the tender bottoms of your feet, and cause you to flinch and hop around like a city girl for awhile until you learn to trust the ways of the old ones.

Our lives are like the uneven ground of the path that leads to the top of the sacred mountain. If we can walk the real path outdoors barefoot, then we will be able to walk the one of our circumstances, and that ultimately determines how we live our lives.

When you remove your shoes to walk barefoot, it is ceremonious and one of the ways we learn to respect the laws of nature. We walk unevenly and on guard barefoot, all the while looking for the obvious because we want to spot the stickers before we tromp on them and hurt our feet.

Paying attention to the obvious is part of looking at the big picture and trying to keep it simple. Although we must look to long range goals as though we were looking up a mountain slope, we must also begin by figuring out how we can get from here to there, and which is the safest path.

Allowing touch to speak

Touch is one of the sacred senses, so we can let our sense of touch guide and speak to us, just as we did on the vision quest when we became acutely aware of how dramatically our senses of vision and listening can guide and inspire us.

We acknowledged our fears on the vision quest, and now we are reminded of other weaknesses because our feet aren't toughened up enough to comfortably walk barefoot on Mother Earth with her thorns, rocks, pebbles, and other matter that makes us uncomfortable. Still, we're curious, and not even a sticker patch is going to stop us. It reminds me of watching a cat stuck in a tree.

Pine trees grow all around the house where I live. Cats frequently climb them, and then cannot figure out how to get down, so they stand there and meow as loud as they can until somebody smarter comes along to rescue them. So like the cat, we are free to ask someone smarter than us to help out when we walk barefoot on our path.

Grandfather knows the way home. If He takes the kids for a walk in the wood, He is also prepared to guide them back in time for lunch. The kids know this, so they go willingly in order to have a good time hiking with Grandfather. We are like the Creator's grandchildren.

Our parents are the Mother Earth and Father Sky. If we are in any way lost, we ask them the way. Mother Earth will always provide a safe path, and Father Sky will guide us to it as we surrender ourselves to life on life's terms.

The individuals of Creation are loving and nurturing elders of the supernatural world. They are there to help and assist us on the path, even when we decide to go barefoot.

Acknowledging defeat

When we reach any turning point in our lives, it usually has something to do with being offered a chance to improve ourselves. Very few opportunities come to us that do not involve some form of sacrifice of self, just as when we walk barefoot on Mother Earth. If we are in business for ourselves and that "great deal" suddenly appears at the threshold of our today, we may find ourselves asking, "How is this going to affect my life?" Will the decision to take the great deal mean we will be forced to work twice as many hours? Is our integrity going to be compromised in some way?

Humility

These questions mean that humility needs to enter our sacred circle, and makes us more cautious. We may have been puffed up about the opportunity given us, especially if we've just completed a vision quest, and think the opportunity is a result of that quest. But once we take stock of what lies ahead, we might not be so sure of ourselves. We will be open and vulnerable, just as we are when we walk barefoot on Mother Earth. Yet, if we choose to walk barefoot, we don't run. We slow down and take our time, all the while trusting that the Creator will look after us.

Maybe we feel that, because we have trusted Creation before and things worked out, we don't need to slow down. This opportunity has been offered to us, and we need to grab it right now! Maybe meditation, watching, and listening are only for those with more time.

Yet, meditation, watching, listening, and touching the earth with our bare feet are the best things we can do with our time when presented with an opportunity of which we're not sure. Humility means that we begin by showing our gratitude. We give thanks for the new opportunity, and ask our own conception of the Greatness of Things or the Creator, to journey with us to the new experience.

Barefoot in the snow ceremony

The idea of standing barefoot in the snow is not a new idea. Some native people honor the wintertime this way in ceremony. If we want to understand humility, we certainly can if we become barefoot on the frozen ground. This is simply a demonstration of our understanding that we are not much without the Power of Creation.

One winter solstice I found myself in the frozen darkness of winter ceremony, a time we honor the purification of the season. It was before sunrise, maybe three or four in the morning, and I had been asked to help tend the fire, which is built hours before the rest of the participants were to arrive. I chose to remain barefoot from the time we lit the fire to well after sunrise, the ending to the time we are in prayer. I wanted to receive the deepest understanding I could possibly receive at this time in my life, which was a rite of passage for me. My actions of faith, standing barefoot in the snow, were my prayer.

I had never liked being cold. It had always been a challenge for me to get all the way through the coldest months of the year without feeling sorry for myself and complaining about how uncomfortable I felt. For example, I had spent more than four years trying to become an accomplished skier, only to give up the sport because it got too cold out there standing in the lift lines. Obviously, I had given up something really fun and exciting because of this weakness of spirit.

At this winter ceremony, I knew that I had to come to grips with something I found unacceptable about myself. During the building of the fire, and dreading the next few hours, I got humble before my Creator once again. Like the cat stuck in a tree, I wanted some outside help. Rather than let any of the nice spiritual Indian people I was with know that I was quickly losing my nerve, I prayed silently for Father Sky to get me through this without making a complete fool of myself. He did! We were nearly out of kindling, so it became necessary to scour the surrounding area for pine cones, twigs, and the like to get the blasted fire burning hot again for the ceremony.

During the business of the moments spent searching for fuel for the fire, I forgot all about my cold feet. The fire roared, and the sun was beginning to appear above the eastern slopes of the highest mountains. Others arrived and the singing began. The songs sung by the men were heartening, and the prayers made me feel warm. Something was happening to me, and I knew it. After standing in one place for nearly an hour, I realized that my feet were not even cold. I looked down at them where I stood a few feet from the fire on the surrounding ice. My feet were below the surface of the ice, and snow atop of the frozen ground was up to my ankles.

I didn't remember the feeling of sinking or anything like that, so I decided to take a step backwards out of the foot holes just to see if I still had feet, or if they had frozen and broken off.

My feet were fine and rich with color, actually looking and feeling very healthy. The place where I had stood for nearly an hour had two foot holes that had melted the ice and gone all the way to the dark earth beneath them. Humility and prayer had provided me with a key to success.

I have memorized a certain way of prayer, and do it every time I find myself in areas of difficulty. It has truly changed my life in incredible ways, as I have repeated it often, sometimes many times a day, over the past few years.

My prayer

> *My Creator, I am now ready for You to take everything about me, all the good and all the bad as You may find me. I pray that You now remove from me absolutely every defect of my character that stops me from serving You and my fellow human beings. Give me strength not to be superior to my relations, but to fight my greatest enemy, myself, and let me know when I get in the way.*

Feeling the earth beneath our feet for understanding

Feeling the earth beneath our feet is a connection with Mother Earth that enables us to discover true understanding, which is otherwise not available to us.

☞ When we walk barefoot on the earth we feel the answer to our confusion on the tender skin of the very bottom of us. We learn to focus on the mountain like a holy man instructed us to do in a sacred gathering.

☞ Letting touch speak guides us the way our listening and watching did during our vision quest. We learn that our universal parents are Father Sky and Mother Earth, and they love us enough to lead us through our own independent actions without letting harm befall us.

☞ Moving slowly is the way to seek wisdom in a good way. We learn patience and silence in the natural world. We learn how medicine people give others the feeling that they are always welcome to be themselves, and that love is the essence of Creation. There is nothing to fear from the bond, which comes from communing with the Mother Earth and Father Sky.

☞ Acknowledging defeat whenever it becomes necessary is how we maintain our spiritual life. It involves taking stock of the things that hold us back. As we approach our Creator with new humility every time we find ourselves in need, we will always get more than we ask for. Humility begins with gratitude for everything we have achieved thus far. And we humbly ask for courage as we move on to the next adventure.

☞ Barefoot in the snow ceremony is a celebration to honor the winter cleansing of Mother Earth. It teaches us how to acquire the needed courage to overcome any weakness we have that prevent us from reaching our highest potential. In this ceremony, we pray for the Creator to remove shortcomings that prevent us from being all we want to become as we move to goals we never thought were possible. We are able to see the activity of the supernatural in our lives.

10

WAYS OF PURIFICATION

Many ways of purification exist, not all involved with physical ceremonies, such as a sweat lodge, a vision quest, or burning sage. Sometimes the purification comes about by the way we view things. We change our perception and become more whole. We purify ourselves even under the most troubling circumstances.

Worthy opponents

Once in a while, someone enters our lives who deserves the title, "worthy opponent." It's as though Grandfather is trying to say, "Okay, let's see what you've got!"

Worthy opponents are people in our lives who are extremely difficult to deal with. They seem to bring out the very worst in us. They put to the test every effort we make to live a spiritual life. They can become one of the stones in our burden bundle (see Chapter 7). We know, though, that stones are our oldest living relations on Mother Earth.

They contain the greatest wisdom that exists in all of time. Worthy opponents are like that. They can become our greatest wisdom, but we usually don't recognize their wisdom at the time. They appear as anything but wise or prophetic.

Most of the time, we judge worthy opponents harshly because of the effect they have on us. They may lie or gossip about us, judge us harshly, or try to steal a significant other away from us. They may even intimidate or possibly frighten us half out of our wits. That fright leads us to the flight or fight response. Our emotions change when they are around. They can steal any sense of self esteem or pride we may have, and walk away looking good while we appear the fool.

The way in which we deal with difficult people is the acid test of who we are and how we use the tools of our spiritual path.

Ways of dealing with worthy opponents

From weakness

- ☞ Hate.
- ☞ Anger.
- ☞ Fear.
- ☞ Criticism.
- ☞ Condemnation.
- ☞ Judgment.
- ☞ Blame.
- ☞ Self-pity.
- ☞ Jealousy.
- ☞ Resentment.
- ☞ Depression (anger turned inward).

From strength

- ☞ Love.
- ☞ Calmness.
- ☞ Praise.
- ☞ Understanding.
- ☞ Acceptance.
- ☞ Honesty.
- ☞ Integrity.
- ☞ Forgiveness.
- ☞ Joy.

Anyone who can push us into an emotional or physical corner challenges us to grow. To understand this is to know that in the spiritual realm no such thing as "victims" exist, only volunteers for the destruction of their own spirit.

When a worthy opponent makes an appearance in our lives, it is time to ask Creation for the courage to change.

It reminds me of a widely known adage, extracted from a longer prayer written by Reinhold Neibuhr in 1926: "God, grant me the serenity to accept the things I cannot change, courage to change the things I can, and the wisdom to know the difference."

Although the saying is known to many cultures, and embraced in many different ways, to me as a Native American, it points to a Creator of all who goes by many different names.

The things I cannot change

Great Spirit would be one way a native might address the Creator. Asking my Creator to grant me the serenity to accept the things I cannot change, is asking that I be granted the understanding that *I cannot change my opponent.*

This is very important information because if we believe that we can change our opponents, we are living in a state of blame. The blame game doesn't work. It only recycles itself a thousand times with the same boring dialogue about us being a victim to someone else's power over us. Blame is like giving someone free rent in our head! If we can understand resentment from this point of view, we're likely to see the futility of playing the blame game. By accepting the things we cannot change, we are on the most important part of the journey to spiritual serenity.

The things I can change

The only person in the world I can change is me. Although it is a concept well established in today's society, it is a belief long held by Native Americans. But how do we come to the conclusion that we need to change ourselves instead of trying to change the opponent who is always too happy to knock us down? The opponent strips us of every ounce of spiritual power we ever thought we could muster. But once we find ourselves in this unfortunate stripped-down state of affairs, we are still able come back to the knowledge that the Creator is there to help us.

For some reason, human nature is much more open to Creation when we feel hurt and vulnerable. So we open our wounded selves and give the whole poisonous problem over to our Maker. We leave our pitiful offering of pain and personal defeat at the altar of our choosing, and ask to be restored, renewed, and healed.

We begin to understand that powerlessness is the doorway to empowerment if we walk through the opening holding hands with the Greatness of Things.

The altar

It is imperative that we do not destroy ourselves with negative feelings for others by moving against them in any way. All the protection we need is in the bond we share with Creation. Anything else is not the traditional native way.

As we walk through our various rites of passage, we learn that our worthy opponent is, by far, our greatest teacher, reinforced by some of the same questions and answers that served us in the vision quest (see Chapter 8). Who are my teachers, and what are the greatest monsters in my life? How do I deal with them?

Turning poison to medicine is the great act of the supernatural in our lives. To bring this about, we need to place ourselves in front of an existing altar—the place where we connect with the greatest Power of Creation. We make sure there is nothing negative in the area near the altar that would weaken us with resentments and fear.

One of my greatest heroes of all time is said to have simply used a large rock that was already sitting outside in its natural environment. An altar is a raised area slightly higher than the floor or the ground on which you stand. I have seen simple tables of altars that reach several stories toward the sky. One friend goes to pray at a place in the wilderness where an Eagle's nest rises high above the rest of the mountain on a windy cold cliff. That sounds like a pretty good altar to me.

We have three altars in our home. One contains icons representing the five main religions of the world, along with American Indian icons. Another holds icons of my private spiritual path, such as Eagle feathers and a shield of a risen warrior on a black horse with a very long mane, in addition to other personal icons. My husband has a personal altar that applies to him alone. My family feels the need to pray many times daily. Our native spirituality carries with it a deep pride of our heritage. We each honor one another's prayers and times of silent meditation. Every room in the house contains spiritual items, because as a family, we feel this is the most important part of our lives.

We also have altars (prayer places) outside. Icons stand in our herb garden and in an area containing a swing to sit and meditate in during warm weather. There are old circles of stones designed especially for healing ceremonies. All of these places are sacred, and used for prayer and devotion.

We never argue about religious beliefs or tribal tradition. We hold only the deepest respect for each other, and place spirituality at the top of our marital promises.

Wisdom

"The wisdom to know the difference" is the last, and most amazing line of the Serenity Prayer. Native American wisdom embraces all religions and beliefs that respect and honor Creation and each other. So, although the serenity prayer does not come from the first nations, it well encompasses the three tenets of true native wisdom as we understand them in many native circles.

Acceptance, change, and wisdom are the turning points in the journey of self into the power of the supernatural, with true wisdom coming only as a gift from Creation.

We can accumulate as many Ph.D.s as possible, and read textbooks filled with all the formulas science has to offer on the nature of our reality, but if we seek true wisdom, we need only ask the Great Out There for it. It will be given in direct proportion to the humility we offer at the altar of the Creator.

"The wisdom to know the difference" is the ability to discern between what we can change and what we cannot. This completely defines the path for us. Nothing is more necessary in human development than the wisdom of the natural laws of Creation. Ultimately, the wisdom of Creation informs us that the things we cannot change are actually none of our business, and only serve to clutter our environment with toxic trash.

Once we're able to accept this divine wisdom, we are able to develop the ancient rituals of communication with the Faraway by following a path of detachment from our most intense worthy opponent. When this happens, all the evil power the worthy opponent once had over us moves out of our arena, and we are free of human intrusion by anyone, no matter what they do.

We take the Serenity Prayer to the sacred altar, and watch as our world comes to life. We learn to fly with the Eagles of our dreams. We begin walking barefoot without trepidation.

Detachment

Detachment is the action or process of separation or indifference to worldly concerns. It is the healing of self, and the ultimate freedom from any type of spiritual bondage. A great medicine woman referred to detachment as not paying attention to what doesn't bring us closer to Creation! It seems too crystal clear in its simplicity to comprehend. It's as if the soul stops playing when it discovers that the things of this world are merely toys. The soul rises above the place of play, and enters the sacred lodge so that it may have nothing more to fear from its enemies.

Imagine Creation as the beloved of our life. The natural world becomes our safest place to be, even when we are barefoot. Creation becomes our favorite companion. If a husband and wife both feel this same way, they have achieved the greatest potential of success in their marriage. In Kahil Gibran's book, *The Prophet,* he talks about the participants of marriage being like the separate pillars of a temple standing near to one another, yet apart, holding up the temple. He also compares the couple to two trees that grow side by side, but never standing in one another's shadow.

When we put Creation first, we receive our strongest source of personal power. It's like being plugged into the highest voltage in the universe that manifests through us all the things we will ever need, including involvement with the activity of the supernatural world.

Sweat lodge

For Native Americans, sweat lodges can be used to heal mental and physical conditions. Natives, being practical, also look to them to heal aching muscles and to cleanse the skin and body.

The sweat lodge is a structure that generates hot moist air, similar to a Swedish sauna. It has been used for rituals of purification, healing, spiritual enlightenment, and contemplation. It can be a small structure with a frame made of saplings, and covered with skins, canvas, or several blankets. Or it can be a more sturdy permanent structure.

Most often, the sweat lodge is heated with hot rocks, with water poured over the stones to facilitate a very intense type of heat. Other methods include a heating duct system with the heat transferred to the lodge from the outside fire. Direct fire method is also used.

Regardless of what type structure is used, they all carry a deep spiritual component that goes along with native belief that you heal only though a combination of body, mind, and spirit.

The giveaway

The giveaway is a purification. It purifies an experience to give something. The native way of the sacred giveaway, or giveaway circle involves sharing a person's skills or talents, or giving material goods that have meaning to the giver, and therefore bestow special meaning upon the recipient. Part of this giveaway, this sharing, can be the stories of your culture.

Other traditional gifts included handmade quilts, jewelry, leather goods, native baskets or pottery, beaded items, and ceremonial artifacts. Today, these same gifts, as well as many others, are used in giveaways.

The giveaway stories

All cultures and ethnic groups have a heritage of traditional stories that make up part of their ancestry. Many of these stories are fluid and continually developing. Your culture's own stories are an important part of who you are.

When native people celebrate a wedding, birthday, or other special event, they give gifts to those invited to the celebration. Often when a person visits a mentor's house, or that of an elder, he or she will bring a small gift.

Part of the sacred giveaway is also storytelling. Our Creation stories spin the philosophical thoughts of our origin. They are filled with wisdom and parables that define human behavior. Sitting around the fire, spinning tales of our travels and those of our ancestors provide interesting and amusing solutions to life's challenges.

When we share these bits of wisdom with others, we attract interesting friends who have wonderful stories of their own. Tribal storytellers from long ago spoke in sign language to other tribes who did not speak the same language. Sign language was mostly universally understood. Much of sign language from a variety of cultures is used today among the hearing impaired.

A good storyteller has always been a fascinating character, and with good reason. Some language scientists and researchers believe that spoken language originated from sign language, and that gestures used today still fire the brain. Even blind people use gestures when they speak.

Our storytellers were and are very animated as their hands move through the signs. Some were very skilled at mimicking the sounds of animals. Young children, adults, and even the very old loved listening to and watching them. They were not afraid to act out every emotional character at its most extreme. It was through these talented performers that Creation stories and other pieces of information were transferred from tribe to tribe, all the way across the Americas. Many storytellers spent much of their time on the road. As they traveled, their stories grew because of the input from people they conversed with along the way. In a sense, they were the first historians and the first mailmen.

As European settlers pushed the American frontier farther across the country, the storytellers tried to stay just ahead of them to inform the tribes of their onward march. As we learn more about ourselves and others, we can be the storytellers of today, just as our ancestors were the storytellers of yesterdays of long ago.

Storytelling is still an effective means of communication, learning, and celebration for a variety of cultures throughout the world and in the United States.

A few years ago, an organization called The Native American Registry for the Performing Arts formed in Hollywood, California. Its purpose was to ensure that only registered American Indians were hired to play the part of American natives in the film industry. They advertised for traditional storytellers to work for movie producers so that the stories in the films did not lose their traditional authenticity.

Scouts were sent to Indian Centers and local reservations in search of native people to fill these positions. Some of us were offered jobs from the Registry. Traditional tribal storytellers were used as technical advisors for many of the Indian films we all pay to see.

It was a step forward in preserving and sharing the traditional stories that are part of our ancestry. And it is the same with your own ancestry. Books and movies often depict the stories of nearly every ethnic group in the United States.

We can all add to this by preserving our own stories in picture and written storytelling.

Gift giving

Gift giving is an expression of generosity. Birthdays and other important days give us another opportunity to serve up our dumplings. Many times we buy gifts for others with the idea that we want to get them something that suits them, rather than sharing a bit of ourselves and our own culture with them. It is pleasing to receive a gift that expresses something special about the giver, rather than the receiver.

A mantle over the fireplace in my home is littered with gifts given to my family from people all over the world, and various parts of the United States. It looks like an altar honoring the different cultures of the planet earth. There is a menorah from the holy land, a tall dark wooden figure carved by an African tribesman, Buddhist prayer beads and candles, sculptured animals from other lands, and statues and symbols from places we have never visited.

It is a beautiful display of diversity, as well as a proud and cherished group of gifts from dear friends who have honored us with the medicines of their own individual identities. Many of these things I had never seen before they were given to us, and the giver always supplied us with a story to go with each gift.

The story is many times more precious than the gift, but the object itself helps us to always remember the history of its origin.

Many ways of gift giving

Working with homeless and unwed moms in my church is one way I can give personal gifts. Lone Bear, spoken of in Chapter 12, shares his gifts of overcoming alcohol addiction, and showing other veterans how to embrace the honor due them for their service so that they may be whole again.

Another man we knew named John had gone through Post Traumatic Stress Disorder, and came to my husband and I for help. After his healing, he shared his experience with others because he believed it was lifesaving.

He also gave my husband a very valuable knife and said, "Thank you for giving my life back to me."

The knife was very special, because John had been a corpsman in the military, and had carried a man out of the combat zone. The man had given John the knife for saving his life.

Years later, my husband gave the knife to a friend of the family, a young man, a U.S. Marine, who was getting ready for his first combat mission in Afghanistan. The family friend is not a Native American, but it makes no difference because these young men are all warriors.

The knife has become part of the circle of power. It has touched many lives, and many parts of the world. It is a true giveaway.

The ways of purification are many

No one way for purification exists. They are many, and some involve a tougher road than others. Sometimes we receive the purification without any preparation, often when it is unexpected. But the result is the same. We learn the truth of ourselves and our surroundings.

☞ Worthy opponents are those people in our lives who bring out the absolute worst in us. We learn how to turn this poison to medicine through prayer and meditation. We come to understand the three fundamental components of our seeking: acceptance, courage, and wisdom. The spiritual thieves who are our opponents become our greatest teachers.

☞ The altar is a place of prayer where we offer ourselves and our troubles to Creation. To do this in a native way, we need to be sure that the place is purified. Sometimes the best altar is just a rock that rises slightly above the ground in its natural environment.

☞ Wisdom is the final frontier of our explorations. It is a gift given freely by Creation simply for asking if the altar is clean and purified. Wisdom gives us the ability to render our worthy opponents powerless over us. It frees us from the role of the victim forever if we are willing to maintain our spiritual path daily.

☞ Detachment is the action or process of separation or indifference to worldly possessions. It is about not paying attention to what doesn't bring us closer to the Creator. We learn that our first priority is the other side of self, the soul. Through this understanding we can develop more passionate and loving relationships with our partners. Everything around us falls into harmony with us and Creation.

☞ The sweat lodge is a way to purify the mind, body, and spirit. It can be used as a single ceremony, or in preparation for other Native American ceremonies.

☞ The sacred giveaway is a purification with another, or with many. When we give, it enriches our encounters, and brings many blessings to us.

11

CALLING THE FARAWAY

Native visions reveal many things. One visionary tells about an encounter with an ancestor who has come to her many times. The ancestry instructs the visionary as she moves along her path to understanding, and tells of four things that can be recognized in physical life, which also exists in the Faraway. They are signs of our spiritual awareness in this life and always.

The elements of Creation

The elements of physical life and the Faraway are earth, air, fire, and water. In other words, after we die, we will still be in the presence of these four elements.

This concept seems interesting and comforting, because when writers try to describe the sacred, they often draw from these four elements to describe their supernatural experiences. In Thomas Dubay's book, *The Fire*

Within, he draws from one of the elements even within his title. Using the metaphor of fire is common in writing that deals with Ultimate Power. Other common metaphors to describe the Great Vision are "Living Water," "Earth Medicine," or "Wind Walker." Those who experience the grace of conscious contact with Creation usually perceive it as accompanied by one or more of the natural elements.

Heat and light also occur frequently during mystical spiritual experiences. Many of those who deal with the supernatural speak of incidents, such as heat or cold, as signs along the way that need attending. Sometimes cold indicates a force to be reckoned with, or a part of the self that needs help. Some of these same characteristics appear to visionaries and others throughout the world, and from all walks of faith or spirituality. And they predate the written word. They appear as one of the common bonds of people who explore the realms of the mystical.

The realms of the mystical, however, are not games to be played by the careless. Nor need they be avoided, even though some people believe the manifestations from the mystical should not be explored. The need is for purification and prayer before entering the journey of the supernatural. We do not go there without the guidance of a spiritual advisor or mentor. Find people to trust and use them whenever they are needed.

Grandfather Creator and Grandmother Moon

Grandfather Creator is the beginning of all life for us. By bonding with Creation, all things of this life give birth to other things. And yet, He has no beginning and no end.

There are as many names for the Creator as there are tribes, such as "The Elder Fires Above," "The Greatness of

Things," "Great Spirit," "Grandfather," "Great Father," and others.

My dad sometimes called Him "The Unknown Order of the Universe," adding that if we wanted to learn about the "Unknown" part of the Order of the Universe, it couldn't be taught or learned from someone else. It was something we had to discover in our own way. Only then would we know for ourselves. He would also challenge us about the way we tried to achieve harmony with the woman Earth He loved so much.

It is the woman who teaches the children about the Creator. She is His mate and the mother of the Creator's children. She is a teacher of spirituality and an original example of the incredible power woman carries, as shown by White Buffalo Calf Woman, who brought the sacred pipe to the people of the earth. Through her example, words, and actions, she taught the people how to pray and show respect to all of Creation, including herself. She was uncompromising in her womanhood. She tolerated no disrespect for her gender, and because of her example, men who understand her were taught to honor every woman they met. The true holy men of Indian country are incredibly respectful to all women.

Women who understand their spiritual gifts have the same responsibility toward men—to show them respect. A woman who walks the path of native wisdom is empowered by the characteristics born into her nature. All the power she will ever need in this life is already within her. It takes many years of proper instruction to understand and utilize the feminine gifts of Creation. That is why we turn to our elders for help in understanding this power.

My grandmother was the elder in my life who explained many of the truths about womanhood to me. One of those was the distractions that arise in the course of a woman's life while she is in her moon. A woman is very powerful during her moon, but it can also make her stressful and cranky. If she is able to journey to a mountain, or get out in nature, she can sort out the thoughts that pass through her and experience a profound spiritual connection with the Greatness of Things.

Unfortunately, many women in the modern mainstream involved in their strongest power of the moon medicate themselves in an effort to make this experience disappear, because it sometimes is uncomfortable, even painful.

Grandmother moon often doesn't fit in with career responsibilities, or the desire for a mellow day-to-day lifestyle. However, the woman's moon is not a mellow feeling for many. If possible, though (and occasionally there are medical conditions that interfere) anything that can affect the natural environment or order of things is best handled naturally, and not with medication because it might interfere with the rich opportunity to receive and record dreams, visions, and other gifts. Remarkable ancient healing knowledge comes to our awareness during the moon time. Creativity is often heightened.

Even when it is not the time of the moon for us, we women need to retreat to safe places for contemplation on the union of our spirit with the Greatest Spirit of all. If we do not live near natural open spaces, we can seek out the parks and gardens of our cities. We can construct a meditative place in our own backyards, in a window box, or make the time to drive to a natural environment.

Women and men each have their special needs, and when we pay attention to those needs, our own and theirs, all benefit from the experience.

What is the personal calling from the Faraway?

The different types of work or vocations are too numerous to mention, but most of us are involved in work of one type or another. But how many of us actually answer a call from a higher place than this earth?

Do we enjoy our job, or are we just laboring for a paycheck? If it is our day off, do we dream about the way we will work when we get back to that job, or do we dread going back to it? Whether we hate or love our jobs, how did we attain them? Did we prepare for them by attending college for many years? Did we work our way up the corporate ladders with or without a degree? Prior to that, some of us took tests in the lower grades to help determine what they were best suited for. Then they went to college and made the desired grades, graduated, and went right to work to establish financial security for their family.

What is your purpose in having a job?

Some folks are driven by material wealth to sustain them in work that they may enjoy or hate. The "top of the mountain" for them is the accumulation of wealth, which is a real accomplishment, and deserves respect. It expresses strength, determination and personal power.

For some, by the time they reach mid-life, they feel a longing for something better or more fulfilling. Does this mean they made a mistake? Certainly not. They just discover they have not yet arrived at he path that calls to them.

A successful psychologist went to school for a long time to attain his Ph.D. In his 40s, he confided that he didn't want to work as a psychologist any longer. It had lost its meaning for him. He was on the red path, and believed that he had to completely change his line of work. He felt he was no longer helping his patients. He knew that the letters behind his name would open some doors to other types of work. But he didn't know how to begin establishing himself somewhere else.

We talked for months about his goals versus his disappointments. As he opened up, he began to discover what he was really made of. I had met him at a writer's retreat where he was the keynote speaker. He had done a class on visualization techniques to improve writing skills. He was a lively, charismatic teacher. He created the lesson plan and gave out colorful handouts to participants. The class was fascinating and useful to those seeking careers as writers.

It was evident from his demeanor while teaching that class (which incorporated humor, creativity, and good eye contact with every student) that he was a natural teacher. He has since studied Reiki healing techniques. Combined with his skills as a psychologist, he has added to his original work by becoming a gifted healer, teacher, and minister of Reiki. He answered his call from the Faraway, changed his approach to a spiritual one, and has become very successful.

Coming to the spiritual path

The years between our late teens and into the 40s and 50s are usually the most financially productive of our lives. As our momentum slows, we begin to consider the years ahead prior to retirement. What does retirement mean to us? Is it a time for stopping and spending the rest of our lives in leisure, or a time to begin something new?

The way we age is heavily affected by the choices we make along life's path. Many people discover a spiritual life as they approach retirement. Spirituality and volunteerism have both shown themselves to be health giving, and possibly add years to our lives. Many retirees choose this path as they leave their careers. Others, however, have been called to dedicate their lives to spirituality at a very young age. Others of us flounder around for many years before making that choice.

The point is that we can come to this spiritual crossroads at any time in our lives. If we feel unfulfilled or a sense of longing sets in at any age, it becomes the best time to explore our spiritual potential. Sometimes a little religion hopping is useful. We open our minds to a variety of ideas in hopes of finding one that clicks. We may visit various places of worship, read books about different faiths, or both. We discover what feels right for us, and what doesn't. Sometimes we return to the faith of our childhood, long abandoned during the career years.

We begin self-discovery at the same time we are trying to answer a call from somewhere deep within and without. We are longing for the non-human spiritual mate that we have never truly met. He is trying to get our attention, and wants to show us a wonderful new shiny path that will add depth and incredible love to everything we already are. Finding that non-human spiritual mate also adds energy, enthusiasm, and strength to everything that lies before us on this journey.

The Creator will add more love and excitement to any existing human love relationship we have, delighting our mate with a deeper meaning of the physical life as well. The Creator does this by shining in our eyes as we bond with him, expressing the love we were always capable of but never knew about.

This is the "Calling from the Faraway." As we surrender ourselves to this call, we begin to discover new skills, talent, and ideas that are exciting to us, and that promise hope and often, new career opportunities. If we stay at our present jobs, we discover new ways of releasing our creativity, and increasing the spiritual territory of our present lives. Our income may increase substantially as well. Perhaps we are already standing in the spiritual arena. Nearly any career can become a place for new light and love to surround us. We may need to make a few changes here and there, but it can be done with the help we are now receiving from the Faraway.

Answering the call

Our call may appear as a desire to do something we have never done before. It can begin with something as simple as a daydream. It often becomes a challenge because we can't figure out how we are to incorporate this desire into our job or lifestyle. This is the time for a spiritual advisor. We can also bounce the idea around with friends. Slowly, we discover that we are able to find small ways to perform the desires of our heart.

We needn't struggle to make these things happen. They will manifest themselves in our lives if our desire is strong enough. We do, though, need to remain open-minded and accept the opportunities that come our way. It is a type of awareness that unfolds before us and that we can grasp if we are ready, if we have developed the self-esteem to accept the awesome opportunities set before us. It is the same with many types of opportunities that come our way. At any age, we must be prepared to readjust our thinking and time for them.

Maintaining a sacred state of mind

It is not a time for standing still when these opportunities present themselves. We can launch ourselves into a course of rigorous action when we are challenged by something new.

Whenever we become excited with a new idea, an opportunity that has landed on our path, we can reset our priorities in parts of our lives that seem set in cement, but really aren't. When these opportunities present themselves, the prayers and meditations that have become part of our daily lives needn't be set aside. Those actions keep us grounded when we stand on the threshold of something great coming into our lives, and all we can see are stumbling blocks.

If we become frustrated and discouraged, it is only a test of how we will handle our fears. Do we really deserve this new set of circumstances. Do we have the time, willingness, and the courage to change? These questions are natural, and necessary if we are to move forward. Questioning helps keep us from going off half cocked like a crazy person. So in our daily communion with Creation, we ask our Creator for serenity, courage, and wisdom.

As we continue to build a spiritual devotion, we are strengthened with the answers that appear in meditation. It is in the quiet time that the gift of sacred knowledge enters our thinking. Trust becomes important. We bond with the best part of ourselves, and to deny it is to waste time. The Creator is not going to lie to us.

Australian Aborigines do an exercise to express trust in their Creator that can put the rest of us to shame. They leave the village for months for a "walkabout" in the wilderness with absolutely no provisions to make the journey safe or easy. They simply trust that as they walk barefoot through the wilderness that their needs for food, water, and shelter will be met. And they are! One observer declared that they must perform some sort of magic, because when they are hungry, food miraculously appears. I believe that it is because these Awborigines simply trust Creation.

Observe the animals to learn trust

Some scientists and others in the literary community refer to tribal spirituality as Totemic. This would indicate that they observe the worship of animals. The truth is, natives do not worship animals any more than those with temples worship statues. Insight into these activities show that just because we see someone praying in front of a statue or talking to an animal, or observing it with extreme concentration, does not mean they are praying to it as they would pray to a deity.

For those interested in learning about the habits and psychology of animals, observe any traditional tribesman. They have a far more complete understanding of the natural world than much of the scientific community, with the exception of those who really love the species they observe. Because indigenous people throughout the world spend a great deal of time outdoors, this is where their best education takes place. If we live outside, it is imperative for our survival to understand the behavior of animals. They teach us.

Part of trusting Creation is to seek the instinctual wisdom of the animals. Animals did not create the earth, but they have developed the necessary instincts to survive in it. Their instincts are incorrupt, unlike those of humans. If we want to know ourselves and our Creator better, we learn an incredible amount from observing animals in their natural environment.

When animals try to figure out what to do next, they remain still and quiet. They sniff the air to acquaint themselves with the nearby surroundings. Before they make a move, they may lower their stance if there seems to be the threat of danger. They proceed with extreme caution. This behavior can serve as a good example of how to go forward in our lives. In human terms:

☞ We stand still and quiet, offering up a silent prayer for guidance from the Creator.

☞ We observe the things around us to determine what we have to work with.

☞ We sniff the air for any danger.

☞ We proceed with caution just as the four-legged creatures do.

☞ We don't stand still forever, though, and neither do the animals.

A family of raccoons lived in an old deserted wood shed about 100 feet from our house. The raccoon family occasionally came on our front porch in search of the cat food they smelled, which delighted our four small children who would "ooh" and "ahhh" at them. They wanted to pet the fat, fuzzy creatures, just as they did the cats. Mama raccoon and her babies seemed cute and cuddly, but our kids didn't realize that a mama creature from the forest in search of food for her young could be very dangerous. Our sheltered human children would stand little chance against a frightened mother who thought she must protect the lives of her young. Our kids thought of us as mean and grumpy parents when we made them stay inside and just watch.

Using your personal power animal

Discovering our personal power animal happens in a number of different ways. We become aware of their existence by paying attention to them, discerning their strengths and weaknesses, and using them in our lives.

When I'm counseling someone who wants to know how they can use the strength given to us by power animals, I usually ask them what their favorite animal is, if particular animals enter into their dreams, or if they encounter them in the outdoors. A power animal doesn't need to be a large predator to be effective. It depends on our own basic personalities. If we choose a predator, such as a bear, mountain lion, or eagle because we have some of their characteristics, we often need to call on other animals for balance. The same can be said for a person who chooses the deer or small birds as his or her power animal. Sometimes they need to call on a predator to get the job done.

One man, a supervisor, was having difficulty dealing with a high-ranking executive at work who was relentless and forceful about getting his way. The power animal of the man I was counseling was a predator, and we determined that his boss was also a predator. It wouldn't do any good for him to use his own power animal to deal with the man because it could injure both of them, when what he was looking for was a solution.

It was decided to use Coyote, the trickster who is also wise. It would be better to deal with the boss using Coyote medicine. Make the boss think he was getting his way, that the ideas the supervisor wanted to implement were actually coming from the boss. It required that the supervisor hold back his own predatory nature, which can create a temporary struggle, but using the coyote medicine, instead, worked.

My own power animal is a predator, because I tend to be forceful and domineering. I can be pretty blunt. One day I was driving down the mountain to go work at a soup kitchen for homeless people run by my church. Sometimes it takes a sort of Army Sergeant mentality to deal with some of the people who come to be served. They can be unruly, argumentative, and hold up the food line, so I had gotten used to shouting, "Move on, move on," and various other tactics to get them moving so we can feed the hundreds of people who come for dinner. As I drove down the mountain, I was thinking about how sometimes I felt unloving when I was so harsh with them, when a deer crossed right in front of my car on the road. It startled me so that my heart began thumping wildly.

I thought about that encounter for the rest of the drive, and decided to use the deer's attributes at the soup kitchen that day. The deer is the epitome of love and caring. It is a gentle animal, not a predator. It gives of itself so that we may eat, and make clothing and shoes for our feet. It wants nothing more than to serve us.

Serving the food that day, I laughed, and smiled, and spoke in a higher, lighter voice. I remembered to give nothing but love, and it worked.

I love cats, and sometimes use them as my power animal. We needn't choose to use our chief power animal all the time. It is there when we need it. Sometimes I have to stand up for what I believe, or what I want, and my personal animal sees to it that I can take a firm stand. Other times that stand calls for a different tactic, maybe a wiser and more gentle one.

The same goes for someone whose chief power animal is like the deer. Sometimes the person needs to call the bear, or the eagle to help him or her through something.

All the animals are there to help us, guided by the Creator. We only need to observe and respect them. Pay attention when they enter our lives, sometimes unexpectedly. They come with messages.

Moving through the circle of our newfound power

The Creator sometimes appears to be a parent protecting us from danger. Maintaining a sacred state of mind involves caution, prayer, meditation, and level-headedness as we move through the circle of our newly found power.

☞ The elements of Creation are earth, air, fire, and water. They are everywhere on the earth and also live in the Faraway. These elements occasionally present themselves along the path we travel into the world of the supernatural. If we think about the "supernatural" as a kind of description of Creation at its finest, we realize that we have simply added the word "super" to the idea of everything natural or of nature.

☞ The Creator, Grandfather Creator, is the masculine part of Creation, while Grandmother Moon is the Power of Creation that pertains to women. She expresses the idea that we must be respectful of every living thing as we embark on any journey into the soul. She is the part of us that holds the most creative instincts, while at the same time being the most destructive force of the earth.

☞ We can discern our personal calling from the Faraway, and make changes in our lives for the better, especially when we discover what is truly important to us. As we move upward toward new goals, it's okay to hold onto those things that we already love in our lives. Our personal calling may manifest itself when we are young, at mid-life, or when we are much older.

☞ By answering the call, we may suddenly desire to do something we have never done before. The way will be opened to us once we open up and allow the opportunities to come to us. We don't need to force anything. Success comes without the limitations we have known in the past when we trust our Creator without limitation.

☞ Acquiring a sacred state of mind means budgeting time in our day for spiritual maintenance. We trust like the aborigines of Australia who do the walkabout.

☞ We proceed with caution on a forward path of self understanding, knowing that not everything we see is actually as it may appear to be.

☞ Our personal power animals manifest themselves in a variety of ways. Study and observe your encounters with animals through dreams, experiencing the outdoors, and by conscious understanding of how they can help us on the red path.

12

WHAT THE ANIMALS TELL US

We are the only species who has been given the ability to create beyond our physical and emotional needs. During the thousands of years of human progression, the animals have remained true to the old ways of survival, which they have always known and practiced. As we watch them, we can see that they seem to have everything they need. They have plenty of food, love, shelter, and a family unit that works for them.

For thousands of years, Native Americans have developed their lifestyles, values, and medicines by following the ways of the natural world. Part of that tradition involves observing what the animals tell us about living a full life. Every living creature on Mother Earth is medicine to us. Sometimes we refer to an animal by its name, just as we might for a friend named Jim, or Sue. Something such as "the wolf," can also be "Wolf."

The following observations are told from the perspective of the animal in a Native American Way. Traditional meanings of animals may vary, often dependent on a tribe's location. For instance, coastal natives may have not been as reliant on the buffalo as Plains Indians.

Buffalo

I am a "giveaway" animal. I am very well aware of my purpose in life. Grandfather has sent me here to provide food, shelter, clothing, and spiritual teaching to the indigenous people. For centuries they have built their teepees with my hide. My hide is also used for their blankets. My meat is nutritious, tasty, and filling.

Indians have always been respectful toward my life and death. They honor and give thanks to the Creator for me. They never take more than they need, and they know that my meat is for their families and not to be sold for profit. Sometimes they come out of the Great Plains just to speak with me. They paint my picture on their homes, and honor me at their most sacred ceremony, the Sundance. I do my best to teach the art of the giveaway whenever they ask.

I show that I am willing to share myself with them. I come here to their homes and stand where they can see me. I willingly offer my life to them, so that their needs may be met. When I speak in the spirit way, they understand that I teach my ways to them. They learn from me to be generous with others.

Deer

I am the totem of love. I lead my relations to the lower slopes of the sacred mountain where they may find the path that leads the way to the top to meet the Creator. He waits there for everyone. There are many paths to the top of the mountain. It is up to each individual to seek the ways of their own people if they wish to meet Him. I am simply here to show love for everyone who seeks the knowledge of His will for them, and the power to carry it out.

I am a very gentle one. I never eat the flesh of others. Many times I am hunted by man, but I am not afraid of losing my life as long as it is for a loving purpose. I simply ask that if you hunt me, you eat the meat and use the hide or give it to a Native American.

A long time ago there was a huge, ugly, frightening demon who guarded the path to the top of the mountain. One of my Grandmothers went to the base of the path. She saw the demon who breathed fire and smoke into her sweet face. He had never met a deer before. He did not know that we are made of pure love, which could not be frightened by evil. His eyes flashed blood red as he roared at her. She just stood there silently loving him in spite of who he represented. He used a lot of energy trying to frighten her and still she loved him.

Loving others is a gentle act, but hating is an exhausting use of personal power. He got tired long before she did, and he began to grow weak. After a while, as my Grandmother stood her ground never moving, he began to shrink. As she watched, she felt sorry for him and loved him even more. He kept shrinking. As the hours passed he became very small. She knew that if she focused all of her love on him that he would completely disappear.

Creator spoke to her. He told her that some people need demons in their lives. He said not to make him completely disappear, but to leave him alone when he had reached the size of a walnut. In this way, the deer has cleared the path for all those who wish to climb to the top of sacred mountain to seek the highest good.

Cougar/Mountain Lion

I am a leader among my people. I am strong and fast. There are few of my relations who can intimidate me. Cautious in every move I make, I have been feared by many. But among my own kind, I am very gentle and loving.

As a parent, I am a responsible provider and teach my young to defend themselves and to hunt with great skill and strength. Sometimes I can be seen wrestling playfully with my cubs in the lazy afternoon, but not a precious moment is being wasted. As we play, they are learning to use their muscles and to defend themselves.

We are warriors who fight for the preservation of our territory. We can be found in wooded swamps, tropical forests, open grasslands and chaparral, brush land, the desert's edge, and the mountains, up to 10,000-foot elevations.

All cats have many things in common. We purr just like house cats. You can take a cat out of its natural environment, but you cannot completely take the "wild" out of the cat. If you watch a house cat, you will see his hunting skills and predator nature. A bit of my kind is in every house cat.

Although I am a feared hunter, I never take more than I need. We eat all that we kill. If you see me in the forest, please do not shoot me because I'm probably just looking for food to feed my family. It is my natural instinct to do this. As long as you leave me and my children alone, I will not harm you.

When you see me, it is a reminder to protect the endangered wilderness, and to follow your own instincts. Care for your family in a loving way, and never take more than you need.

Bear

I am the great silent dreamer. During the cold months of the year when a blanket of virgin snow covers the Mother Earth, I sleep. My heartbeat slows from 45 beats per minute to 10. This is when I enter the silent mystical place of dreams. I dream for the entire winter. No one on the mountain dreams as long as I do. I have great visions of truth while the purification of the season rests upon the quiet, frozen slopes.

When you see me in the warm spring, remember to look inside yourself to see your dreams. With the bear as the symbol of your dreams, you will be able to understand their true meaning. Look at me and honor the introspection which brings intuitive sacred knowledge.

In the wintertime, if you are quiet and respectful of the forest, you will not wake me. When you honor me in this way, I will come into your dreams and share with you the secret knowledge of your heart. You will come to understand the purpose of your individual path on this earth and my power will give you the strength to carry it out.

In the springtime, the native people will have a gathering deep in the hidden wilderness and dance to wake me up. They are the dreamers of the humans and they honor their healing visions. Around a huge blazing fire, they dance in a circle wearing the skins of my brothers. They sing for me and pray to the Great Sprit for my survival from the icy winter slumber.

We hear their drums and wake from our sleep. To many, I show myself dancing in the smoke above their sacred fire. Many times we gather at the edge of the woods near their ceremony and sing back to them. When they see me, they smile and say the words of gratitude.

Raccoon

I am the keeper of scrutiny. I examine every wonderful thing I can get close to. I have slim black fingers on my front paws which are very dexterous. It looks like I am wearing leather gloves. I scratch myself with my fingers just like you do. Everything on the planet is interesting to me. I am very inquisitive. I want to know how everything works and what it looks like on the other side of itself and inside.

If I see a flat rock, I want to know who lives under it. My purpose in life is to learn everything I can about everything around me. If you leave your things lying around outside, I must examine them carefully. I might even need to take them home with me. Grandfather gave me a black band around my face, which looks like a burglar's mask. That is so you will know that I just might take some of your things if you don't put them away.

If you are lucky enough to see me, you are reminded to pay attention to every detail. Do not accept anything at face value. I am here to teach you about caution and scrutiny. Examine your motives and the motives of those around you. Your life is sacred and important. Guard yourself and watch closely what you are doing.

Stay close to the ground and never jump into anything without learning everything you can before you proceed. At nighttime, you see things a different way. The forest is quieter and more peaceful. Try to look at things from a serene point of view.

Skunk

I am the keeper of sacred defense. Do not come too close or I will spray you. The defense I keep is unique. It is important that each of us understand who we are and what we must do to survive. If we are aware of the gifts which our Creator has given us, then the world is a much safer place to live. My spraying is the way I protect myself. It is not there to offend you, just there to let you know that I want you to keep your distance.

I am here to remind you that you must know who you are. We are all vulnerable creatures. And we are all important to each other. Everyone is here to be of service to others in some way. I am trying to teach you to look at yourself and everything you have been given by your Grandfathers. Perhaps your talents are very different from those of others. Or maybe the things you don't like about yourself are the very things that can be your greatest gifts. Did you ever think of that? Perhaps they are your best defenses.

If you are unhappy with anything about yourself, reexamine the things you question. I am a lesson in acceptance. If we all just respect each other and mind our own business, everything will happen just the way it is supposed to. Respecting other creatures and others of our own species is the essence of honoring Mother Earth.

Porcupine

I am the giver of quills. I am a loner who gives away my protection for the beauty of the arts. For more than 1,000 years, native people have used my quills for many beautiful works of art. They are woven into moccasins, dance regalia, and many other fine garments that are worn proudly by Indians. Natives used to kill porcupines just for their quills, but today they corner the animal and tap the back of the animal with a Styrofoam paddle to collect the quills. The quills are dyed with locally obtainable vegetable materials and then sewn into skin clothing, earrings, and artistic items.

When I am old and go over from this life, my quills will live on for much longer than my people. We are not killed for fun or greed. When we die, we live on in respect and honor.

If you see me in the mountains, remember that the creative gift you give others is of great value. Perhaps the gift is a kind word or a gentle look, or smile given to someone who is having a bad day. Perhaps your gift is a painting or a song. Remember that joy and beauty live on long after you have gone to the Faraway. Every gift is important in a world filled with many problems.

Your gift could be as simple as giving your seat to someone who looks tired on a crowded bus. The awareness that you express is your creativity. It is the artwork that endures for thousands of years. It is the love of all Creation.

Beaver

I am the home builder. I build my home along streams, lakes, and ponds where the air is clear and water runs eternal. I can cut down large trees with my sharp teeth, as big as 30 inches across. I use them to build my lodge with sticks and mud. My home is strong, warm, and safe. I have learned that I am happy when I live where I am best suited, according to my unusual talents and gifts. I am proud of who I am and proud of my fine home.

When you see me at the river, remember that your home is a place for you to build with honor for yourself and your family. It is a sacred temple of healing and love. It is the place of protection. You and your family will be strong and healthy if your home is secure. Use the gifts of your environment to improve your living conditions. Everything you ever need is provided by the natural world. You are the keeper of your people, and the maker of your own empire.

Become grateful for the shelter of your lodge and the strength of your species to provide a safe and loving home. Surround yourself with things that nurture you. Keeping a good home requires continuous work and improvement. Each year, make it better. You will prosper when the chill of winter winds challenges your foundation. Every day, take time to appreciate your own efforts to make it better.

Use every part of yourself to provide for the prosperity of yourself and those you love. You will be able to do this when you build a home as secure as mine.

Horse

I am known for carrying the people to their desired destination. Many times, natives ask me if they may cut some of the long hair from my tail. I tell them I would be honored to have them use my hair in the making of their spiritual symbols. They say they ask Creator to help them to reach their goals and destination. Every time they look at the horse hair on their clothes and regalia, they remember to have faith in their Great Sprit.

For thousands of years, we have served humans in many ways throughout the world, and in the Americas since the 1500s. Creator put us here to help you to arrive wherever you need to go. We have carried people over huge hot deserts, mountains, valleys, and golden plains all over the world. When you could not travel so far into the wilderness, we were always there to help.

Native Americans blended their spirits with ours in ceremony. We ran together, conquering the buffalo to feed the tribes of the Plains. Children's eyes brightened as they were placed on our backs for the very first time and we carried them gently around the arena.

Whenever you see one of us, be reminded that there is always a solution to carrying your burdens. Great Spirit will never leave you stranded without help. Look to your four-legged relations with faith. He has prepared a way for your travels no matter where you need to go. You may cut a small piece of hair from my long tail to carry with you. Let it remind you that there is always help nearby.

Eagle

I am a symbol of courage and power because of my size and superb aerial skills. I build my nest in places that are unreachable to most and they are sometimes 6 feet in diameter. There my young are born in the solitude of this high place. I am the second largest bird of prey in North America, and I am endangered.

My many cousins of different names and sizes can also be found throughout the world, and they have been honored by many cultures.

The Golden and Bald Eagles are the most revered in North America. My body is about 3 feet long, and I have a wingspan of up to 7 feet. I fish when I am in flight because my eyesight is so good. I can swoop down from great heights to catch my prey. I can be found near lakes, marshes, sea coasts, and rivers.

The native people find me fascinating because I fly so high that my feathers touch the Creator, which is their oldest living relation. My feathers are sacred to them, and they use them when they pray. Natives believe that the feathers carry the spirit of the Creator and that to own one of them is a great honor.

I represent enlightenment and spirituality. Many believe that I come to them from the east where each new day begins. I bring the promise of hope and good fortune.

If you have problems and feel the weight of heavy burdens and you see me flying above you, understand that your troubles will pass. They are harsh lessons of this life. They are not there to hurt you, but rather to teach you. Begin to think of your burdens as challenges. Move through them with the courage to change.

Learn to look up when seeking self-improvement. There is a world of incredible beauty where the treetops meet the sky. I am the guardian of your spiritual path, no matter how you see the Creator, or by what name you call Him.

I will show you how the planets circle the sun in perfect harmony. If the sun is high in the east, perhaps you will glimpse the hope that comes with each new sunrise.

Turtle

I am one of the oldest life forms on the planet, dating back 100 to 200 million years. I was here long before dinosaurs. To Native Americans, we represent Mother Earth, because of our age and our ability to survive in the cruelest of conditions. But like the earth, we cannot last forever.

Some of the native clans are named after Turtle, and Turtle shell rattles are used in the ceremonies of the medicine people. Our painted pictures appear on beautiful ancient pottery. Stones combined with silver have been sculpted with honor depicting Turtle. We have been respected by most of the North American tribes. The Iroquois say that when the earth cracks, the turtle is stretching.

Each lifestyle, from farmers to nomadic hunter-gatherers and everything in between, has had different social and religious expressions, but all are based on the life-giving sources of the natural world. Perhaps the next time you see me, you will remember that this sacred planet is your source of life and home.

Squirrel

I am a tree dwelling gray squirrel who eats nuts, seeds, fruits, and plant material such as pine cones. I have a keen sense of smell and can find a store of foods buried deep beneath the ground 100 feet away. I am a gatherer and a vegetarian. I communicate by tapping my front paws and verbally chattering. My friends and family and I chatter from treetop to treetop all throughout the woods.

Some of my smaller, far-flung kin live in the deserts, near oceans, and on the prairie. We also sometimes live in people's backyards in the city. We are many different kinds of breeds.

We lived in all of these places long before humans came. But once they did come, such as when native people came to the mountains, we taught them how to gather protein rich nuts and store them in warm snuggly places for winter. We also showed them where the tastiest ones were. But if they didn't hide them good enough, we'd dig them up, and then they would hide them better the next time.

Native people learn much from the animals who live in places near their homes, and they still come today to gather the nuts. They use them for nourishment and healing.

Snake

I am the keeper of senses. I have developed my senses far beyond the wildest dreams of most humans. I also teach others how to walk away from the past without looking back. I do this by shedding my entire skin from time to time. Periodically, we all get tired of who we are.

The question is, how many of us are willing and completely able to let go of old habits and move on to a more youthful beginning in a brand-new shiny skin?

When I become uncomfortable with the ways that have become no longer acceptable, I get cranky and irritable. Most folks do. I do not feel like eating or playing or being nice to anyone. Do you ever feel that way? When that happens to snakes, you will hear a lot of hissing and warning signals. We want to strike out and bite someone. Some of my cousins are equipped with a rattle that lets everyone know just how they feel. We have been created with the natural medicine of willingness to change. If more humans felt that way about changing their old ways, the whole world would be better off.

We begin to wiggle around within the old skin. It itches and no longer fits the way it used to. Letting go of the past is extremely uncomfortable, but we are not afraid of that. We are brave about change. When one is willing to let go of the old dysfunctional past, the sky is the limit. We just keep moving forward until the pain has passed and before you know it, the old, used exterior is behind us.

After we have walked away from the old skin, our senses are sharper than ever. Focus is my finest magic. Focus on what you want. Like me, if your heart is good, the Creator will make sure you make use of your senses, and help you change if you really want to change.

Wolf

I am Wolf, the teacher of the animal kingdom. I am extremely loyal to my family. The example I set is one of loving leadership to my pups and their mother. This loyalty brings great rewards of gratitude and affection from those to whom I am closest.

I am an esteemed leader among the other animals wherever I roam. My reputation is far worse than my reality. Humans are afraid of me. Let it be known that a healthy wolf has never attacked a human.

Most native people have felt for thousands of years that wolves are their brothers. That is why it has never been acceptable to hunt or eat us. They knew we were related to the dogs who pulled their sled and travois and lived among them.

We live within our circle of power for every season of the year so that you may learn from us. We are most often spotted during the twilight hours of dawn or dusk. We are a symbol of the free unspoiled wilderness. We live by the rules and are ritualistic guardians of sacred mountains.

If you see me among the pines and boulders, remember, do not be afraid. I am here to teach you that you must observe the most honorable of all human characteristics. These are loyalty to your family, rituals, guardianship, and honor.

Guard your home and family. Live by the laws of the planet along with all the wilderness around you, and respect the ancientness of your race and the homeland of your ancestors. Be an example of honor to all Creation, and protect the things you know to be true and sacred.

Rabbit

I am the epitome of the giveaway. I am gentle and small and eat only vegetables, such as herbs, tree bark, and other greens. I never harm anyone or anything. I am very timid and shy. If you come upon me, I most likely will be running away, because I am so easily startled. That's because my hearing is among the acutest of the animals.

Native Americans have hunted us for a very long time. They always thank us for giving our lives as their food.

Their gratitude is much appreciated by us. Our hides are used to make many useful things. Sometimes, we have been available when there were no buffalo around.

If you are lucky enough to catch a glimpse of me in the wilderness, remember that the giveaway of love is the most important part of happiness and self-worth. The best way to forget your problems is to help someone else who is in need. After you move from this life into the spirit world, you will be remembered for the love you gave to others. My life is for teaching you this sweet lesson.

Whale

I am the keeper of ancient knowledge. I have an extremely large brain that remembers everything. Our slow graceful movements through the depths of the blue silent oceans represents the conscious awakening of introspection, creation, and song.

We live in very deep icy waters so we have been provided with blubber that is sometimes 20 inches thick to protect us from the cold. We are linked to sound by the fact that we operate by sonar sensitivity. Our own song is like no other you will ever hear. It has been recorded by man to enable him to relax and look inward for answers to his living problems. Our gentle sounds are a singing gift of timeless knowledge for the world to enjoy.

If you see me swimming gracefully in the ocean and shooting water from my spout, enjoy the vision of tranquility and silent grace. Look inward to the center of your soul for sacred truth and protect your creativity with a layer of silence, as the blubber protects me from the cold depths of the ancient ocean.

Remember that only in quiet solitude can you discover the timeless knowledge of the universe. You are welcome to my mystical songs, which can carry you far away from the stressful grind of daily living. Use the sacred songs of your soul to weave solutions for the survival of mankind, the whale, and Mother Earth. This is the essence of your inner creativity and the ancient knowledge that resides deep within the heart of every living thing.

Butterfly

I am the keeper of four lifetimes. I begin as an egg where I sleep within the circle as I grow. After that I become a larva. I live close to the ground and look something like a worm. I must walk everywhere I go and that portion of my existence teaches me humility. Once I have reached an understanding of humility I become a chrysalis. This is when I sleep, grow, and dream of being a butterfly.

Before I emerge, I have grown to hundreds of times my original size. In my chrysalis, I totally transform. My internal systems completely reorganize while adult structures are developing. After a while, I break free of this cocoon and as my wings unfold, I discover that I am an entirely different type of individual. This is how I have become the symbol of transformation. When I emerge, I can fly! The changes that have occurred in my identity provide me with the knowledge of my purpose in life.

I have come to this world to give color, joy, and life to all the flowers. I illustrate that we must all bring life and color to one another.

Understanding the changes I must go through in the course of my life teaches you to accept the changes in your own life.

I am the gentle greeting from the Faraway who comes to tell you the sweet secret of the universe. Today's problems are but a speck on the continuum of all time. You are only in the beginning of eternity. This life is but a learning process so that you may come to understand all things. The answers to every question are already within your heart. All you must do to find them is follow your own heart, be patients, accept change, and hang on. Soon you will know the freedom of the butterfly.

Lizard

I am the keeper of the shadowland. I do not sleep when I am very still in the afternoon heat. That is when I am seeing the dreams in a waking state. This talent sharpens my senses. By being perfectly still and focusing all of my attention, I can feel the vibration of Mother Earth and my eyes can detect the most subtle movement. I have the ability to move silently between our material world and the Faraway.

I am also the keeper of detachment. Although I use my tail for balance, I am willing to let go of it if someone grabs it or steps on it. This teaches humans that sometimes we need to let go of a part of ourselves to which we have become accustomed. If that part of us becomes something which can cause harm or death, it is time to let it fall away and begin to grow another new part to replace it.

The next time you see me and I seem to be resting, remember that I do not waste one second of stillness. Did you know that a large part of success in any area is based on your ability to remain detached and develop your perception?

If you listen to your own perception in silence, you will surely notice things that other folks miss. You will become psychic and intuitive in a way that can change your life. Do not waste one moment of stillness.

Owl

I am the keeper of the darkness. I can see nighttime as few others can. I am also known for wisdom and healing. I am a nocturnal bird of prey who feeds entirely on living things.

Many times I am considered related to the moon. Some folks even think I am a bad omen, but this is not true. My mystical nature frightens those who do not understand it. Even Native Americans of different tribes do not agree on the significance of Owl. The reason is that nighttime is somehow associated with the darkness inside all of us. I do not represent your darkness. I represent understanding all parts of your spirit, even the parts you would wish to deny.

Night vision is the ability to see through deception. If we are seekers of the light of purity, we must not be fooled by deception and lies. My gift to you is the strength to be courageous even in the face of fear. Fear is an illusion that can stop you from reaching the top of the sacred mountain. It is your inability to see in the dark.

Because I can see at night, I can assure you that there are no more dangers than that there are at midday. I also have a very keen sense of hearing, which enables me to accurately discover where the things I want are located. My yellow eyes bring the color of the light of the sun into the night. If you seek the understanding of Owl, you will possess the medicine of hearing what others are trying to hide. This will protect you from being deceived by those who wish to harm you.

The greatest enemy we face is ourselves. Discover the ability to look within yourself without fear. When we face the demons that hide within our souls, they lose their power and we become enlightened. This will provide the greatest healing for the planet and for mankind.

Raven

I am the keeper of the magic of Creation. I am at the peak of my creativity during the winter. My mystical nature exists because I bring the medicine of change. I bring forth life and order and can help you understand the language of all animals. I am also intelligent and can be taught to talk. We can even imitate the sounds of other birds.

If you see me, remember that you have the talent to access spiritual laws as well as the laws here on Mother Earth. Learn to understand the teachings of all animals and to communicate with them as I do. Imitate the songs of others, and be willing to accept change in your appearance or habits whenever you need to. Be as flexible as the willow who bends its branches willingly with the winds of change.

You have the opportunity to learn new talents and skills every day and to enjoy every moment of it. It is a magical experience to become someone new and have all the exciting experiences of that unique individual. I bring messages from the spirit world for you. You can take that which has no form and give it life with your own creativity. Do not be afraid of change. Take a risk and look for the magic in the outcome.

If you stand in a dark place in your life, understand that the dawn of a new you is near. Don't push it away. Embrace it and you will find out that you are about to give birth to a being. You are about to understand the secrets of Creation like you have never understood before. You are becoming ready to bathe in the sunrise of a new beginning.

Spider

I am the Grandmother who weaves the web between the past, present, and future. On the silken thread of my design rides the traditions of the indigenous people of this land. Those who carry the ways of their "old ones" into the present are the keepers of the web. I weave the original language of Turtle Island.

I teach you to stand between the east, south, west, and north with balance in the center. Stand between man and woman, black and white, water and air, and hot and cold to find the balance between the opposites. Become centered. Let the life force flow through you from the sky to the earth and be perfectly still. Weave the language of your people in silent communion with nature.

I awaken creativity within you. Become the center of your universe. Do not become fragmented. Be still and grounded, and begin your creative skills from there, working outward from the center toward your goals in this life. Do not focus on the successes of others. Focus on your own accomplishments, and the solutions to any roadblocks you may encounter. The solutions will set you free from getting trapped in the webs of others.

My silken web is the dream catcher. The delicate network of fine threads allows the sad times to pass through the web and back into the sky, while Spider holds the good dreams of the ancients for all those who wish to keep them for today and tomorrow.

Coyote

I am the trickster. I represent the playfulness and wisdom of the animal kingdom. It would take years of walking my path to even begin to fully understand me. I adapt quickly to any living situation. I am very smart. I use the ingenuity of the skills of others to help get the job done, because I can find the shortcuts in every task. On my path, anything is possible. The balance between playfulness and wisdom is delicate, but you will do well to master it.

One of the things I am best known for is my haunting howl. I may be expressing a fear of danger, loneliness, or calling for help when I am howling. Most people stop to listen when they hear me, because the sound appeals to their wilder nature and the roots of their ancestors. Some are even frightened by it, because they most often find themselves far removed from the natural laws of Mother Earth.

When you see me, there are many things you can learn about yourself. Ask yourself some questions. Is someone trying to trick you, or are you trying to trick yourself in some way? Are you taking life too seriously? If you are, you are out of balance. Learn to pay attention to the motives of others. Find the playfulness in serious situations.

Develop an understanding for great wisdom, but remain flexible and adaptable to every living problem. Remember who loves you and be grateful for them. Be loyal and help others discover playful wisdom. The tricks in your life do not represent cruelty on the part of Creator, but rather a lesson in adaptability. Dance out of harm's way and move into the sunshine of gratitude by making a list of all the things you are grateful for.

Focus on the solution. If you do not know what it is, find out. Start by being good yourself.

Hawk

I am the messenger from Creator. I represent power, enlightened vision, and protection. The way I fly and hunt, and my acute eyesight are symbols of power and mysticism, because I am much the master of my own destiny. This is a trait that many would like to possess. I can lead you to your life's purpose by guiding you in the vision of higher understanding.

I can be seen perched on top of telephone poles or treetops where I use my keen eyesight to locate prey. You can learn from this: observe the world from a higher place while resting and watching.

I have the talent of soaring in great circles in the sky where I am sometimes attacked by smaller birds. This can show you that if you have the ability to soar to great heights yourself, many times others will try to attack your abilities as well. Be watchful and careful of jealousy from other folks who feel less than you.

The spring and fall equinoxes and the new moon are my greatest times of power. If you see me, perhaps you need to look to these times if you are about to make some kind of important change in your life. These seasonal changes are important because they represent letting go of old habits, and the birth of new times and opportunity.

We hold the key to higher consciousness and balance between beauty and harmony. Those who choose astral projection as a spiritual experience many times learn from Hawk. The idea of spiritually rising to the greatest heights of the heavens and soaring to new awakenings is what I can teach you. Conscious contact with the universal powers of Creation leads to greater development of your personal power. Your highest achievement is dependent upon discovering your most profound energy levels.

If you see me, remember that Creator is trying to get in touch with you, and I am His messenger. I bring the positive message that your path is right and good. You are going in the right direction. Reach upward to the spiritual places of the sky, and the mystic laws of your highest self.

Oyster

I am the keeper of solutions. I represent perfect alignment with the learning process of all Creation. I have done more than any other living being to illustrate the use of the problems in our lives. Problems are not really problems, but are challenges or opportunities that are gifts from Grandfather to enhance our lives.

Someone opened me up and took a good long look at what I have done with adversity. I create a pearl from a grain of sand. Many have tried to make pearls, but no one can duplicate my original design.

A minute particle of foreign matter enters my shell from time to time. When that happens, I begin to coat it with layer upon layer of nacreous material. This makes the particle less scratchy to live with.

When a pearl necklace is worn by a woman, it is said that it enhances her greatest beauty and displays prosperity. These beautiful pearls were created by my inability to withstand the pain of my problems.

If you are given a natural pearl or you see an oyster, remember to turn the poison in your own life to the greatest medicine. Creator has given you the natural ability to do this. All you have to do is take the time to discover it. All of your problems are given to you to learn from. They are gifts for you to attain the wisdom of the ages. Nothing happens without a very good reason. If you handle a seemingly negative intrusion as an opportunity for growth, you will reach your highest potential.

A long time ago, I was given a nice hard shell to protect me from all things that could hurt me. I always thought that would be all I would need until the day something got inside. Just about the time you may think you have it made, the world can deal you what appears to be a nasty blow. I am here to remind you that a solution and a purpose is in everything, even pain.

Dog

I am the most loyal animal. If you take me into your heart when I am very young, I will stand by you until the day I die. I will always let you know when there is danger nearby with the racket I will make. When everyone else has let you down, I will still be your best friend. I truly care about everything that happens to you.

We are related to the great wolf. He was our first grandfather and teacher. You can see a bit of Wolf in me. My teeth are similar to those of Grandfather Wolf. I still have many of his hunting skills with my sharp hearing and keen sense of smell. But the look in our eyes is different. I posses far greater skill at tail wagging and bonding with humans. If I live in your house, I will always be there waiting when you come home. Don't forget that you hold the highest place of honor in my life.

Dogs come in every shape and size you can imagine, and we are of use in many different ways. We help blind people and serve in the military. Sometimes we pull sleds in the frozen winter in places such as Alaska. We sniff out drugs for law enforcement officers, and protect junkyards. We are the most economically dependable alarm system folks can buy.

We are helpful animals. I am letting you know about honor and respect, which are the great gifts given to us by the Creator of all things. Try treating others with a more loyal attitude. Stand behind those you love and there will always be plenty of food, love, and shelter in your life. Be an example of love and loyalty to others, and to the Mother Earth.

What the animals have told us

Although many more animals exist throughout the world, the ones presented here offer insight, answers, and solutions for all of us. It comes to us just by observing them, and by using our deepest intuitive powers. We learn from them by instinct and intuition what we can't learn from other humans, because the people around us are wrapped up in searching for their own ways to deal with the problems of living as a human being on this planet. It is doubtful that the animals would turn to us for answers to their problems of living and seeking the right path.

☞ Buffalo: Share the good of you with others.

☞ Deer: Seek the highest good on your path.

☞ Cougar: Protect what you have, but honor others.

☞ Bear: Honor your dreams and visions.

☞ Raccoon: Examine yourself and everything around you.

☞ Skunk: Respect others and mind your own business.

☞ Porcupine: Express your creativity by giving to others.

☞ Beaver: Fashion a harmonious home and take care of it.

☞ Horse: A reminder that the Creator will help to carry your burdens.

☞ Eagle: Hope comes with each sunrise.

☞ Turtle: Take care of the sacred planet. It is your home.

☞ Squirrel: Learn the ways of the natural environment.

☞ Snake: Focus and trust your senses.

- ☞ Wolf: Respect and protect the ancientness of truth, your race, and homeland.
- ☞ Rabbit: Help others in need.
- ☞ Whale: Discover the timeless knowledge of the universe in quiet and solitude.
- ☞ Butterfly: Life is a learning process, so be patient.
- ☞ Lizard: Learn by listening and watching and remaining detached.
- ☞ Owl: Look within yourself without fear.
- ☞ Raven: Do not fear change.
- ☞ Spider: Be the center of your universe, and do not become fragmented by getting caught in the web of others.
- ☞ Coyote: Find the playfulness in serious situations, and examine the motives of others.
- ☞ Hawk: Seek always your highest self.
- ☞ Oyster: A solution and purpose exists in everything, even pain.
- ☞ Dog: Respect and serve others with loyalty.

13

PURPOSE OF THE POWWOW

An attitude exists among many native people today that says:

I am alive, and I am here! I have endured the many changes history has presented, and I have survived! Look at me. I have a gift for you. It is all that I have, but it is yours. You may embrace it and keep it as your very own. It is the ancient songs of Brother Wind. It is the dance of the Grandmother River over time-worn rocks. It is the supernatural sight of Eagle with Father Sky, and the healing medicine of Mother Earth.

Powwows and ceremonials

Centuries before the arrival of Europeans to the Americas, powwows and similar ceremonials took place among tribes throughout the continent that gathered together to trade with one another. During the gatherings, they danced, prayed, sang, and shared tribal foods and stories.

Natives have always known that trade took place between Indians from throughout North and South America, with routes running the length and breadth of the continent. These routes are still being discovered.

The powwows enabled various tribes, or traders from those tribes, to share with one another in joyous celebrations. But they also had other purposes. The word "powwow" originated from an Algonquian word meaning "conjurer," because they also took place to cure disease and to ensure success in hunting and battle.

Regardless of the original reasons, good powwows today require four main components (some of which were required in pre-Columbian time):

☛ Traders selling handcrafts and other goods from their individual cultures.

☛ Food booths featuring native foods dating back to pre-Columbian times.

☛ Proud displays of dancers in bright traditional regalia.

☛ Native music that revolves around the drums and singing.

The rhythm of the drum, round brown faces with extraordinary dance outfits knit the union of communal bonds on the crowded powwow circuit. Dancers compete sometimes for big prize money in various categories. Often divided into age groups, dancers earned rights to participate in a certain dance, wearing certain types of outfits. For instance, some dances may be for young, single females only, and others for well-respected traditional dancers who have been honored with sacred Eagle feathers.

Although most dances are not done for prize money, they all carry significance for certain tribes, groups, areas, or seasons. Different areas of the North American continent are noted for particular dances. Natives from desert areas, particularly New Mexico and Arizona, may specialize in dances honoring rain and farming. Natives from colder areas of Nevada, Utah, Oregon, and California may perform a special dance to ask for enough food to see them through the winter.

Today's powwow affirms old ways and celebrates the reunion of old friends who have known one another and shared the old ways for generations. It provides young people with a chance to meet and show off native skills of dance, and other highly respected talents, such as drumming.

The familiar sights, sounds, and smells of the powwow never change much from gathering to gathering. Once, driving on the freeway with the family to meet friends at the Sherman Indian High School Spring powwow in California, we could hear the drum as we approached the off-ramp to the school.

Another time, after receiving an invitation to a powwow at a college campus, we drove through roads lined with classroom buildings, and turned a few corners, but were experiencing difficulty locating our people. Finally, one of the kids in the back seat caught a whiff of burning sage, and shouted to my husband, "Follow the smell, Dad." Pretty soon, we all smelled it and were able to follow the scent to a small dirty path leading up a little hill. We parked the car, walked up the path, and found everyone assembled and preparing for the opening ceremonies.

Heartbeat of the earth

The drum, whose rhythmic resounding beat provides the measured steps of the dancers, is sometimes called the "heartbeat of the earth." When women step into the center circle of the powwow to dance, something magnificent happens. Our own heartbeat joins with the pounding cadences of the keeper of the sacred medicines, who is our Mother Earth.

We become united in harmony with everything natural and ancient. The pride of the great warriors and the gentle beauty of our grandmothers joins us as we dance in traditional celebration of everything our heritage says we are. With every step, we feel the belly of Mother Earth beneath us sending strength, courage, and native pride coursing through our bodies. We feel it from the souls of our feet to the top of our heads.

Foot-long fringe at the bottom of my dance shawl moves with the pounding of my heart in union with our mothers, grandmothers, and the life-giving women who have danced before me. My daughters dance in furious circles around the matrons of my people, blending brightly colored regalia with the wind to brag of the beauty of our young, strong children.

During the dance, I reaffirm to myself that no place exists where I would rather be today, and no more love have I ever known than the enduring living culture of our land.

We dance to the songs sung by our husbands and sons where we meet together in the lodge of our Creation. Hawk circles the powwow grounds to tell us our celebration honors all our relations in a good way. And so the medicine of our ceremony comes to life again as we gather to dance and sing of who we are, just as we have done for decades during our moving, living heritage.

The beat of the drum becomes even more a part of our own heartbeats, and enables us to share the very pulse of life with the stories of Creation. Young men's voices blend with the rivers of the mountains, and the fire of the sun that brings the corn to life. We know we are loved.

This heartbeat is the who and why of us. It is the rejoicing of our unity, and our life-giving observance to the Greatness of Things that is the source of everything right and beautiful.

Somewhere in the far-off wind, the Sundancer blows the eagle bone whistle, and we gather around the northern drum where we receive the culmination of our strength as one people celebrating life together. Now the beat is deeper, stronger, and its intensity renders us to stand within our universe as though we are the center of almighty Creation. We are linked now, and bonded with all that ever was, is now, and ever will be of us, world without end.

I see my husband standing at the drum and joining the songs of honor and unity. My son is pounding out the heartbeat of a warrior. We are family, and the blood of our people sings strong. We are the wind and the mountains and the deserts of America. We are the first and the last of this land, and we have never been more alive in all of time.

Welcome to the heartbeat of the Mother Earth, and the songs of celebration of the two-legged. This is the celebration of the intertribal powwow. It is generally open to anyone who wishes to learn about, experience, and share in the heritage of the American Indian.

Presentation of the Eagle staff

From an opening in the east of the circle, we enter into the dance, led by an honored military veteran who carries the Eagle staff. This is the "grand entry," or the first of the opening ceremonies of the powwow. The staff is held high, and can be called the flag of the native nations. Every dancer who proudly wears the regalia of their place in the grand entry follows the staff into the huge circle that has been blessed by sage and prayers. Every item used in the ceremony, such as the drums, drum beaters, hands and heart of the singers, and all other objects of the music and dance have been prayed over in the old ways. All spectators are asked to stand and respect the staff and Eagle feathers worn by the dancers.

The Eagle staff may belong to one of the elders who helped to prepare the gathering. It is dressed with sacred symbols from tribal tradition.

The Eagle staff can be 6 or 7 feet tall. Many times it is made of willow. The end is curved to form a semicircular top. It is shaped like a shepherd's staff, and just as the shepherds' staff is used to lead the four-legged, the Eagle staff leads the two-legged in the beginning of the ceremonial.

It may be wrapped with the fur of an animal, and with ribbons representing tribal colors, or the four colors of man: red, yellow, black, and white. Tied and hanging from the staff are Eagle feathers, possibly representing the number of gatherings the staff has represented. Each staff is unique. Its individual "dressing" is the result of an elder's visions.

As the Eagle staff enters the arena, it is carried at an angle so that it proudly displays the feathers of the sacred bird. Behind the staff, three flags are carried: the American flag, the state flag in the center, and the POW-MIA (prisoner of war/missing in action) flag on the other side. The latter is to honor our fallen or captured native warriors who have willingly defended this sacred place of our birth. The Eagle staff expresses our native purpose and courage as the first nation to stand in defense of our land of heritage.

Grand entry is marked by a flag or honor song as a tribute to the purpose of the powwow. Usually elder men enter first, then male dancers, followed by elder women, then women dancers. Teens and children follow next. Dancers also enter the arena arranged according to the category of dance they represent. The categories range from a few to several different classifications and purposes for a particular style of dance. The different groups of dancers are determined by those arranging the intertribal nations powwow. The number can also reflect the size of the powwow. Some are very small, and others, very large, such as the annual Gathering of Nations Powwow that takes place in Albuquerque, New Mexico.

Come talk to the Eagle staff to bring her to life. Honor her and she will honor you, and she will give you the strength and courage to guide you in your path. Touch the staff and feel the medicine and take the strength of the Eagle feathers into your heart.

These words were said one year by the one who led prayers for an intertribal gathering in Albuquerque, New Mexico. They describe the spiritual interaction of the chosen native dancers with the icons of their culture.

During the grand entry, all those attending stand with hats removed, the same as when the American flag passes on other occasions.

Prayers by the elder

All songs at powwows are performed in a native language. After the honor song, a holy man offers the prayer of invocation. The one praying usually prays in his own tribal language, and then again in English. He prays to the Creator, giving thanks for everyone who made it safely to the gathering, and showing gratitude for all the creatures of the earth, and the blessings that come with being a traditional native person.

The elder then asks for purification and blessings to be given the dancers, drums, and everyone involved in the powwow. More often than not, the selected elder is a well-known and respected elder whose many relatives are involved in the dances and songs of the gathering.

Some of the dances

The dances are one of the main attractions of a powwow. They are filled with symbolism, ritual, practice, preparation, and respect. Most of the dances are separate for men and women, and also for age groups. If during the dancing, an Eagle feather were to fall from a person's regalia, the dance and drumming stop, and the audience stands until a feather has been returned properly. It is a very solemn moment because the Eagle's feather is sacred. Some believe the Eagle feather is a symbol of warriors from the Faraway.

Most of the larger powwows today invite non-Indians to participate in certain intertribal dances that are announced.

Men's Southern Straight Dance

The Men's Southern Straight Dance has been referred to by some as the "gentlemen's dance." The regalia is characterized by a porcupine headdress, or an otter cap and otter trailer extending from the dancer's neck to the ground. Each dancer, in harmony with the slow-paced beat of the drum, imitates the hunter, watching the ground, searching for tracks of prey.

Dancers must listen closely to the singers to maintain the correct interpretive mood and to end on time. Expressions on the faces of the dancers should complement the spirit of the hunter's story.

Men's Northern Traditional Dance

Passed down for centuries within the northern tribes, the Men's Northern Traditional Dance features regalia of leather, a feather bustle, and bone breastplate. Each dancer dons his regalia and moves in his own style. He dances the spirit of battles and hunts, lost in time, but kept alive in the tradition of this dance.

Men's Fancy War Dance

Brilliantly colored outfits and two feather bustles characterize the Men's Fancy War Dance regalia. Dancers follow the rhythm of the drum with their steps, the motion of their heads, and the flow of their bodies. The steps are individually determined, so the expression of the emotion of the music and the change of pace from the slower northern style to the faster southern beat are important. The dancers are judged by their fast footwork, originality, and the beauty of their regalia.

Men's Grass Dance

The Men's Grass Dance is considered one of the most ancient dances. The regalia is characterized by long yarn or ribbon fringes, which move to the rhythm of the dancer's body. The motion of the dancer should cause the flowing regalia to move as if it were blowing grass on the prairie. It should be danced in perfect time to the music, responding as the grass does to the motion of the wind.

Women's Buckskin Dance

Regalia for the women's Buckskin Dance is made entirely of buckskin, decorated with beaded designs and long fringed sleeves. Discipline is essential to the slow, graceful movement of this dance. Dancing in perfect harmony with the drum while never breaking the sedate spirit is the dance's essence. The dips and sways are executed with no break in dignity.

Women's Cloth Dance

The regalia and the expression of the women varies by tribe for the Women's Cloth Dance. Buckskin or cloth leggings and moccasins are beaded. Other bead work and intricate ribbon designs decorate the regalia, which is often complemented by beaded necklaces. The dance is one of dignity, an attitude that must be maintained throughout. Judging includes the ability of the dancer to stay in time with the drum, create a sway of the shawl, and stop in time with the drum.

Women's Fancy Shawl Dance

Beautifully designed bead and ribbon work characterize the regalia worn in the Women's Fancy Shawl Dance.

The elaborately designed shawl is an integral part of the regalia. Each dancer has her own style, so how well the steps and motions express and harmonize with the drum is most important. Though the dance involves more motion and agility than most women's dances, the grace of the woman is always expressed.

Women's Jingle Dress Dance

The Women's Jingle Dress Dance regalia is made of cloth embedded with hundreds of tin cones or jingles. It has made a tremendous comeback in recent years. Although many legends exist on the origin of the Jingle Dress, I was told that it evolved at Milacs Lakes Minnesota around 1919, when a young Native American girl was given a Jingle Dress when she was 10 years old, after being told by her grandparents that it originated from a dream. Instructions for making it were given in the dream. It was considered a healing dress by some tribes.

Regardless of its origin, it is one of the more popular dances today, with a variety of different songs, beats, and steps that make it necessary for the dancer to distinguish which dance is appropriate. A Jingle Dancer must be able to vary her performance with the pace of the drum, whose beat can be changed at any time by the singer.

Bear Dance

The Bear Dance is done to step back in time to a purification experience of mystical reverence for the power of the natural world where an open mind is essential to true understanding of the ceremony and the Great Spirit.

The Bear Dance is a social dance, traditionally held in the spring with slight variations among different tribes. For some tribes, it originally began when the first thunder of spring was heard. It centers on a purification experience through dance, stories, and song (often originating from individual dreams experienced by the person during the long winter months). Today, it is widely used during spring powwows, many of which are open to the public.

Bear medicine of any sort helps to make a person strong, and is often evoked for the aid and protection of Bear spirit.

Today and yesterday

The purpose of today's powwow celebrates a Native American's heritage, in addition to making many of them available to non-Indians, so they can witness and enjoy what the powwow has to offer. Hundreds of powwows throughout the nation are open to the public.

☞ For the Native American, a powwow is an opportunity to visit old friends in an environment that expresses the pride of natives, and a chance to worship together under the direction of the elders as we have done for eons.

☞ The ceremonial drum unites the heartbeat of the earth with our own hearts and those of Mother Earth and Father Sky. It is a sort of audio-icon of our bond with the natural world, the Faraway, and the oldest people of our tribes who have passed on. The rhythm of the dance is in harmony with all things of Creation that we feel as we enter the powwow's arena.

☞ Presentation of the Eagle staff marks the claim we stake on the sacred circle of the arena. The staff is the flag of the native nations. It is brought into the arena to signify the beginning of the grand entry of the ceremonial powwow.

 Following the presentation of the Eagle staff and the Flag Dance, the prayer by the elder is given in his native langue and in English for all of us to have a successful powwow and the blessing of the Grandfather Creator.

 The dance descriptions tell of the various styles of men's and women's dances, which are commonly performed at powwows. Most of these dances have been around for a very long time, and in some way lend significance to the prayers and dreams of the people.

 The Bear Dance, performed at some spring powwows, is a purification ceremony filled with mystical reverence for the power of the natural world.

14

HONORING THE MILITARY

Native Americans have honored their men and women who have served in the military throughout the years. We believe it is one way to develop inner strength, valued throughout our history, not only as a warrior in battle, but in other areas of life. By serving on the battlefield, wherever that may be, our warriors feel honor and respect from our people. Once having fought on the battlefield, a warrior knows the Greatness of Life.

War record

Native American men in the past have served in nearly all the American wars, including service on both sides during the Civil War; the Spanish American War; valiantly in World War II; during the Korean conflict in the 1950s; and in Vietnam. They were never forgotten by their own native people. But some, who drifted away from the old ways and had no contact with their families, elders, or natives on reservations did not receive the proper honors due them. Nor did they receive honors from the non-natives with whom they came into contact once the conflict ended.

Our people have also served in Grenada, Panama, Somalia, Desert Storm, and Afghanistan. We have served proudly in special units, such as the Navajo Code Talkers, a group of approximately 400 Navajos who served during World War II. Their special language helped the United States send messages in codes that were unbreakable to opposing forces.

Changing times

Throughout most of our history, with rare exceptions, it is the men who have served as warriors, and it was they who were honored by all. Some Native American groups still hold to the old ways, and honor only male warriors in special ceremonies, but that is changing now that warfare has changed, because more women are serving in every capacity in the military.

Because of this change, a few women are now honored by carrying the Eagle staff at the opening ceremonies at powwows. The Gourd Dance Society, still limited to only male veterans, will before long, probably include women, according to my husband.

My own daughter is now serving in the military, and I am glad to see these changes, although I'm still not certain about how to respond in a native way. I was raised and taught in the old ways. My husband, who is a veteran, speaks more of the newer ways of honoring those who have served in the military, including women he has seen carry the Eagle staff.

Traditions for warriors

Our traditions hold that our warriors need and deserve healing and purification before and after going into battle. Therapists at veteran's hospitals dealing with Post Traumatic Stress Disorder following the Vietnam conflict have praised healing through the sweat lodge and other native rites.

Purification and healing on a personal level involves fasting, songs, giveaways, and sweat lodge ceremonies, as well as family gatherings with special and personal welcomes home.

Other honors follow the warrior throughout his life, such as becoming a member of the Gourd Dance Society and carrying the Eagle staff at powwows (see Chapter 13), honors that are only offered to veterans.

Gourd Dancers

The Gourd Dancers, all veterans, perform prior to a powwow, so many non-Indians don't see the ceremony, although sometimes all are invited to watch the dancers. Traditionally, it hasn't been a big attraction to outsiders because the regalia is not so colorful, and it more subdued than the dances seen during the powwow. Once invited to become a member of the Gourd Dancer's Society, veterans must be trained by an elder for a year to become a dancer.

The Gourd Dancers wear black pants, black boots, a long-sleeved white shirt, and a blue and red vest or a sash holding the man's military insignias and any medals he may have earned during the wars in which he served. These include everything from the Bronze Star to the Purple Heart.

They purify themselves before every dance event with prayers to the Creator, by observing and honoring the directions, and with smoke from sage, cedar, or sweet grass.

The steps of today's Gourd Dance resemble those of the Sun Dance of the Kiowa, once outlawed by the U.S. government along with all tribal religious dances and ceremonies. The Gourd Dance came out in public again in the 1940s when some Kiowa elders performed it for the American Indian Exposition. Since then, the dance has grown in popularity.

The songs of warriors and others who have gone on are preserved within the songs of the Gourd Dance. During the first song, the dancers remain seated and shake their rattles in time to the song. At a certain point in the song, usually during the beginning of the fifth start, the dancers rise and dance in place. They shake their rattles and flex their knees in time to the drum beat. During the middle portion of the song when three hard beats are introduced, the dancers makes a slight bow and take small steps toward the center, but the they usually remain close to the same place until the end of the song.

The gourd rattles carried by the dancers keep rhythm to the drummers and singers from the Southern drum, which is lower pitched than the Northern drum.

They dance sometimes with the wife or daughter standing behind them, but the women dance in place with a shawl.

Opening a powwow

A veteran usually carries the Eagle's staff for the opening ceremony at powwows, and other native functions. It is carried side-by-side with the American flag, and holds much the same meaning. The staff has, in the past and now in the present, inspired patriotism the same as the American flag does for native and non-native alike today.

It is usually wrapped in buffalo hide, and contains eagle feathers, and sometimes horsehair, sweet grass, sage, and strips of red, white, yellow and black cloth to honor the four colors of humankind. Blue or green is sometimes also added. As with the U.S. flag, it should never touch the ground, and people should stand in its presence.

The various staffs throughout Indian country, which are never mass produced, are usually kept by a veteran's group, or tribal elders. Native Americans have always honored their warriors, and will continue to do so.

A warrior's story

When a warrior is distanced from his or her native traditions, it can create havoc in their lives, especially when battles are fought, leaving confusion in the mind of the person, as in Vietnam. Many of those warriors, Indian and non-Indian, returned to face hostility in their own country instead of being honored for the service they had performed, usually at a very young age when they are still experiencing their rites of passage.

Lone Bear was one of those warriors, a U.S. Marine. He had never embraced the traditional old ways, and returned from Vietnam a bitter and despondent person, albeit with a bag full of medals, including the Purple Heart. On his return, he hid his medals.

He also joined the growing list of veterans who suffered from Post Traumatic Stress Disorder. Alcoholism soon joined his distress.

My family met Lone Bear when he came to visit his father who lived in our small community. His father was Native American, but didn't practice the old ways. He sent

Lone Bear to see my husband and I so we could help him interpret a dream. In this repeating dream, he kept hearing Indian drums, and seeing Eagles fly over a rocky mountain.

I pointed out the symbols of his dream as they related to Native American spirituality. The thought intrigued him, and before long, we slowly directed him toward a Native American path. When he went back to his own home in another state, he sought out an elder and took part in his first sweat lodge. It turned out to be a profound experience for him.

By the time he came to visit us a year later, he was using the sacred pipe in the old way, and the year after that he was making his own pipes in the old way. He became more amazing each year he returned to visit.

Eventually, he carried his numerous medals in a wooden chest lined with velvet. They were beautiful, and something of which to be proud. He had been ashamed of those medals, but through his healing became proud of them, as well he should have been. He eventually realized that the medals were part of his spirituality. He is deep into the old traditional ways now, his voice and attitudes are softer. He is coming into his eldership.

He now devotes his time to helping others, which is part of the giveaway. People love him. They follow him around like puppy dogs. He's very kind, and is of service to his people.

Honoring our military

All military men and women need to be honored, not only for their present military duty, but for that of the past because it becomes the heritage of all of us.

- ☞ Native Americans have fought valiantly to ensure the freedom of U.S. citizens in all of the country's wars.

- ☞ Although male warriors have always been honored in Native American culture, some groups are starting to honor the women warriors who are now part of the military.

- ☞ Native warriors receive purification from their people when they return from battle.

- ☞ Warriors are honored at powwows and many become members of the Gourd Dancer's Society, open only to military veterans.

15

YOUR HOME, A SACRED TEMPLE OF HEALING

The most sacred place of all within the circle of life is our home. Just like the circle, there should be no "sharp edges." Teepees, hogans, and wikiups were round with no dark corners to clean, but their roundness isn't all that we mean by "sharp edges." By sharp edges, we mean anything that makes us frown or feel bad when we come in contact with it through any of our senses. Dark corners are those places where things are hidden and made useless by their hiding places. They are like the dead, and carry only weight within them. They need to be recycled. Holding onto useless objects is like living in the past. They create what Native Americans call "a burden bundle" (see Chapter 5).

Burdens around the home

Like old grudges and other burdens, these objects in the dark corners of our homes become like old grudges and other burdens. They tie us to the lowest part of ourselves, weighing us down and creating lethargy that dampens our spiritual energy.

Our houses, physical and spiritual, need good cleanings periodically. If we remember that the first residents of this land were, to a great extent, hunters and gatherers, then we must know the value of traveling lightly. Another characteristic of many natives is that we were nomadic. We traveled with the seasons to higher and lower elevations in search of the most nurturing environment.

Today, we stay mostly in one location, but we see the wisdom of living in the now, and not hanging onto things we no longer need, or that may have been unnecessary in the first place. Just like prayer, the simpler our lives can be made, the more effective they are. So we look around the home to find the things we no longer need, and pass them on to someone who can make better use of them. At the same time, we sharpen our awareness through prayer and meditation, so that our lives will also be lighter and unburdened.

During a search throughout the house for unneeded objects, we look for dark medicine of which to be rid. We may believe such objects are priceless antiques, or objects that have come down through the family. But if they appear "dark" to us, other relatives may feel differently about them, and make good use of them.

It isn't that these items are bad, it is rather that they are not right for us because our instincts tell us so. We can look around our homes and find the objects that just don't "feel right" to us. We don't even need to understand why we feel that way. We just need to move them out. My husband and I have some items in our home that are good to us, but that spiritually conflict with other items in the same room. We may only need to move them to another location that does not contain items that conflict. Once moved, either to another room, or to another home, the objects will again contain positive energy.

It is a lesson in trusting our instincts so that our homes become a sanctuary, or safe place for us to return to each day to heal, rest, and refuel.

Stimulating the home environment

Like the animals of the sacred mountains, we can instinctively hone our skills at living, with the colors, smells, sounds, and an individual ecosystem with which we surround ourselves. An important part of spiritual growth is to develop an awareness of all our senses. Awareness itself can nearly be considered as one of the senses, especially when we want to make contact with supernatural forces.

Color

If we are the extremely active type who has trouble relaxing, we may try surrounding ourselves with cooler colors in an effort to subdue ourselves a bit. Lower or indirect lighting is good for the overactive spirit. Color is actually pulsating energy. Colors affect people differently because when we are exposed to certain colors, our reaction depends on our current mood, the surrounding noise, and the temperature.

The chromosomes of the body also help determine our reaction to certain colors. For example, the body's cells are more responsive to red than to blue, because the chromosomes in the body are more adept at "seeing" red than blue.

Generally, however, blues, deep greens, and grays used together produce a calming effect. If we tend to be depressed or lethargic, we aim to boost our energy with warmer colors that stimulate the metabolism, such as violets, pinks, oranges, yellow, and red. For passive-aggressive types, those who seem unruffled and non-demanding (but who usually get their way), darker earth tones help to level out their not-so-hidden tendencies.

Aromas

To understand aromas, test a few types of candles and incenses to discover which ones foster a sense of well being, and which ones make you irritable. Certain aromas are said to produce different feelings and moods, and this may be true. But I believe it is wiser to use aromas that personally please us.

In the home, however, it is important to not offend other family members who may not share the same aroma sensitivities. For example, my favorite aroma is frankincense, but my husband is allergic to it. So when I crave this aroma, I burn the resin outside. My husband and I, however, both love the smell of sage, which we also use in Native American ceremony. But my daughter is allergic to the smell of sage, so until she became an adult and left home, we didn't use sage inside the house. We always kept any ceremonies that called for sage outside.

Music

Music is also a powerful component of our home environment. We are heavily influenced by the music we hear, just as we are by the sort of friends with whom we associate. Research published in the Annals of the New York Academy of Science in 2000, among other studies, indicates that different types of music affect immune, nervous, and endocrine systems.

As we listen to music, it's more important to discern how we feel about the music than whether or not we "like" it. Do we feel relaxed, excited, angry, depressed, spiritual, energetic, playful?

Our internal bodies react to everything we encounter on the outside. The steady beat of a Native American drum, which is nearly in rhythm with the heart beat, and the rhythm of the universe can be very calming.

But not all music need be calming. Some music is for dancing, other for engendering patriotism, such as the wealth of patriotic music we heard in the aftermath of September 11, 2001. It made us feel as if we were a part of something bigger than ourselves, and we felt camaraderie with others.

Music is not an inconsequential thing.

Our own ecosystem in the home

What is the most wonderful and memorable place you've ever been? Was it near water, in the mountains, the beach, out in the middle of the desert, or in the heart of a busy city? If we wanted the best possible vacation, where would we go? If we went on a quest, where would it take us? Where does your heart take you during a daydream?

During a visual journey to a desired destination, go back for a minute or two to the front room of the house in which you live. How can you bring the elements of your dreams or vision to that room? What were the colors, smells, sounds, and other sensations of your vision?

The family room in our house contains an aquarium, because my husband and I love water and the sound of water. The fish tank is it's own small ecosystem. I watch the fish swimming around, eating all sorts of things off the plants and the bottom of the tank, bringing to mind the immune system where T and K cells roam around consuming junk that needs to be taken out of the body as waste. This comparison may follow me as the result of too many college classes about the human body, stemming from a major in medical science.

The immune system becomes an icon to me when it involves decorating my own home. Icons are an image or figure that represents something, such as the icons we use on computers that when clicked, open up to larger materials or pictures. Icons can serve as symbols of another place to which we would like to progress.

Spiritual icons are reminders of the places we seek in our spiritual and psychological lives. So we surround ourselves with things from our experience that nurture us spiritually. We place them in the rooms of our homes the same way native people painted the icons of their lives on the interior walls of their teepees.

Our home is our refuge from that part of the day when we are out in the world competing, working, standing up straight and being "socially acceptable."

At the end of the day, we can walk through the front door of our home into colors, aromas, sights and sounds that are going to heal land purify us.

Icons

Native Americans decorate many of our everyday tools. Looking around any museum with native artifacts on display, it's evident that they express the colorful cultures of their origins. The beaded handles of knives, the woven designs on baskets, and the blankets and other items used in the tasks of daily living, all reflect the prayers and priorities of their makers.

Many of the pictures depict icons of spiritual or psychological knowledge that comes with the rights of passage. How many of the kitchen knives we buy have beaded handles? How many department store blankets have the signature and power animals of their weavers depicted on them? How many of the baskets and jars we use illustrate an artist's rendition of the spiral dance?

Making the home a sacred temple of healing

If someone decided that the tools used most often in our lives need to carry stories of who they are, why shouldn't our homes? Our dwelling places can be made into sanctuaries of spiritually, nurturing and healing.

☞ To make the home a sacred temple of healing, begin by removing anything that doesn't feel right.

☞ We pay attention to colors, shapes, aromas, and music.

☞ Only keep stimuli in the home that nurtures us on the red path.

☞ We always show respect for other members of the family by consulting them about any needed changes in order to serve the highest good of all the family.

☞ Instincts are the natural drives we are born with.

☞ We may not be able to control the ways in which we may be forced to survive, such as the type of work we do, so we need to meet our physical needs, such as food, clothing, shelter, and love in the home to keep us healthy in mind, body, and spirit.

INDEX

About the Authors

Fran Dancing Feather is a writer, editor, teacher, artist, and natural health consultant. After receiving her B.S. Degree from Clayton College of Natural Health, Dancing Feather began teaching Methods of Natural Healing, Science of Natural Healing and Circle of Relations (how to discover ourselves through animal medicines). She also provides personal consultations for healing through herbology, mind-body work, spirituality, and 12-step work.

She has worked as the spiritual advisor and consultant for the Big Bear Writer's Retreat; spiritual consultant for Native American Women's conferences; retreats for women in recovery; Indian Health Services; she is the facilitator for Substance Abuse Ministries, and works with Native American Ministries at St. Joseph Catholic Church in Big Bear.

Rita Robinson is a former health and psychology reporter, now full-time writer with more than 1,000 articles in magazines on four continents, and author of 11 books, including another on Native American practices. In addition to cowriting *Center of the World* and *Exploring Native American Wisdom* she has had articles published on Native American culture.

Robinson has appeared on radio and TV in connection with her published work, and has been quoted as an expert in newspapers and magazines such as *Martha Stewart Living*, and *Weight Watchers*, for articles on friendship, palmistry, caregiving, suicide, and being single with class. She guest lectures for several organizations, associations, and libraries.